THE MODI DISRUPTION

Advance Praise

'Over the past decade, Prime Minister Narendra Modi has reshaped India's governance and political landscape. Moving beyond the typical focus on economic reforms, this book explores how PM Modi has transformed governance at a grassroots level, making a meaningful difference in the lives of ordinary Indians. Arjun Singh Kadian does a commendable job of capturing these changes, illustrating how PM Modi's initiatives have reached households across the nation. It is a consequence of these interventions that Modi remains a formidable force in Indian politics. Engaging and fast-paced, this book is a must-read for anyone seeking to understand how PM Modi's impact on ground reflects in his unparalleled electoral success.'

Anand Ranganathan, author and scientist

'The decade-long journey of PM Modi's governance has been a testament to Bharat's remarkable quantum leap in progress and development. The book seamlessly navigates through Modi's evolution from his roots to his current stature as a global leader, delving into history, politics, and power dynamics along the way. Arjun presents compelling arguments and well-substantiated facts, demonstrating how Bharat's trajectory has been fundamentally reshaped by PM Modi's visionary leadership and unwavering commitment to development and transformation.'

Baijayant 'Jay' Panda, member of parliament and author

'From the economy and diplomacy to narratives and culture, Arjun's Singh Kadian captures the ongoing rise of India being crafted by Prime Minister Narendra Modi. *The Modi Disruption* is a well-researched book that binds disparate strands of Bharat's transformation into a singular narrative.'

Gautam Chikermane, vice president,
Observer Research Foundation

'This is the chronicle of how one of the most consequential political leaders of Indian history transformed India. More than the shiny new infrastructure or improved global standing, writer Arjun lucidly tells us the story of how Prime Minister Modi changed the way Indians thought of themselves as a people.'

Sanjeev Sanyal, writer and economist

THE MODI DISRUPTION

India in Transition

Arjun Singh Kadian

ink | OCCAM

ISBN: 978-93-6547-735-1

First published in India 2024
This edition published 2024

BluOne Ink Pvt. Ltd
A-76, 2nd Floor, Sector 136, Noida
Uttar Pradesh 201301
www.bluone.ink
publisher@bluone.ink

Printed and bound in India by Thomson Press India Ltd.

Kali and Occam are imprints of BluOne Ink

ink | OCCAM

The Wheel Turns for India

Modi is no Lodi[1]
Obsessed with tombs and cenotaphs
He'd rather leave behind
A tabled growth on graphs

He's waking up a nation
Half inert and dreaming
He's shaking up our patience
With bureaucratic preening.

Disruptions now make history
Like bloody wars once did

With freedom fighters' blessings
Now Amrit rains our lands
The wheel turns in Karma
And rolls on in Dharma

The multiplier effect isn't
All about breeding
There's IT and AI and
Young India beaming

Modi is no Lodi,
Obsessed with death and afterlife,
He's disrupting the disruptors
With self-propelling strife.

—Aman Nath, October 2024

---

1 The Lodi dynasty (1451–1526) of the royal Afghan Sunni descent were the fifth and last dynasty of the Delhi Sultanate, remembered more for its wars and tombs than its productive contributions.

Contents

ACKNOWLEDGMENTS

I believe it would be fair to begin by thanking Prime Minister Narendra Modi for steering Bharat to the path of progress, which was hitherto hazy for many Indians. Through his daily actions, he has motivated and inspired countless young Indians like me to devote themselves to the service of the nation. It is a consequence of his uncountable efforts that people like me are witnessing the transformation and documenting India's transition. So, thank you, my prime minister.

One can agree that we all stand on the foundation laid by many stalwarts before us. I truly believe this. In fact, it is these legends, mentors and friends who believed in me and nudged me into writing. I thank each one of you wholeheartedly. Thanks and regards are also due to Sanjeev Sanyal, Smita Prakash, Baijayant 'Jay' Panda and Gautam Chikermane. Thank you, Aman Nath, for being a constant source of wisdom and encouragement.

In addition, I'd like to thank Ranjit Gupte, who was particularly enthusiastic about this story. In addition, I would like to thank Ajay Kashyap for his insights into the development of sports in India over the last decade, and Aparna Phadke and Rajesh Singh for their perspectives during the development of this book. Thank you, Alok Bhatt, Shiv Mishra, Monica Verma, Manvendra Singh and Rahul Kaushik.

In addition, I thank the Prime Ministers Museum and Library, Delhi, for its support with resources and facility to develop this manuscript. I would also like to thank my publisher Praveen Tiwari for his trust and efforts in fine-tuning the manuscript and Thanglenhao Haokip, senior editor, for managing the editorial process.

Most of all, I would like to wholeheartedly thank my parents, Mr Gunvir Singh and Mrs Anita Kadian. Thank you for everything. I am because you are! Thank you, Anirudh Singh and Suranya Sur. Regards are also due to my in-laws, Mrs. Shuchi and Mr Ashok Sur. And a very special thanks to my friend and wife, Suhelika. Thank you for your patience, faith and support as I work endless hours for causes far more significant than myself.

AUTHOR'S NOTE

Why did I write this book? It's a fair question to ask. After all, if there are clean public spaces, a vast network of multi-lane highways, mobile penetration and connectivity nearly everywhere, airports in tier-2 and tier-3 towns, fast and modern trains, direct benefit transfers done digitally to beneficiaries linked to Aadhaar cards, electricity connections to the remotest villages, toilets in nearly all rural households, and more ... all of this is to be expected in a country that gained independence more than seventy-five years ago and has been democratically ruled by governments committed to public welfare. Where is the need to blow the trumpet on such achievements, one may ask.

Those who have seen and lived through those past decades will understand the huge transformation that we witness today. The new-age generation will likely take what it has today for granted. This book chronicles the dramatic changes that have taken place and how they have impacted the lives of people, especially the marginalized and most vulnerable sections of society. I feel it is important to document some of these developments so that we as a people—and the readers—understand and appreciate the context: in short, where we were and where we have come.

First-time voters in 2024 would have been around ten years old when Narendra Modi took over as prime minister in 2014. They would have little idea of what the state of affairs was back then. The economy was in free fall, scandals of corruption in high places had become the new normal, the internal and external security situation had turned precarious, and the targeted beneficiaries of government schemes rarely received what was their due—a large part was siphoned off by middlemen. Not having experienced those times, first-time voters of 2024 were especially susceptible to false narratives that were promoted through social media and other channels of information.

As I worked on this book, I realized how convenient it was for people to forget the positives that had happened during the last decade; after all, public memory is said to be short. As the Opposition continued to promote falsehoods, the Modi government's achievements were not just taken for granted but also played down by sections of the public.

This book, therefore, is an attempt to capture bits and pieces of the remarkable story of India's turnaround in the last decade. While there were several initiatives that were taken over the years, I have tried to cover the major developments that came with the rise of Modi: infrastructure development, health and sanitation, education, the economy, direct benefit transfers, reaching out to the Indian diaspora, the evacuation of Indians from crisis situations from various parts of the world, and women empowerment through a slew of measures are some of them. The themes were selected for the impact they showed over the last decade.

As the year 2024 began, the country was gripped by election fever. But there was another important development that seized the imagination of all Indians. It was the inauguration of the Ram temple in Ayodhya and the consecration of the Ram Lalla idol on January 22. Prime Minister Narendra

Modi led the consecration, and the event was watched live by millions of people not just in the country but outside too. Celebrities from various areas of activity attended the high-profile event. It would not be an exaggeration to say that the entire country was awestruck, and the eyes of millions of people were glued to their television screens. It reminded one of the days when the streets would empty as the serial *Ramayan* was telecast on Doordarshan.

Many political commentators observed that, in a way, the function had set the tone for the elections. It was obvious to all that the Bharatiya Janata Party (BJP) would return to power with Modi at the helm; the debate was only about the number of seats the party would get. As the election campaign got underway, picked up steam and its impact was projected in the media, including social media, it became obvious that Modi's opponents had launched a vicious, negative, and false propaganda against him and the BJP. In those early stages it was not clear how it would affect the electoral outcome, but most experts believed that the impact would be minimal.

As it turned out, the BJP fell short of the simple majority mark. It suffered a major setback in the crucial state of Uttar Pradesh and underperformed in Maharashtra, Haryana, and West Bengal. However, it did tremendously well in Odisha, where it swept both the Lok Sabha and the Assembly elections. Also, the National Democratic Alliance (NDA), of which it is a major component, outdid its rivals in Andhra Pradesh in both the Lok Sabha and the Assembly polls. The BJP opened its account in Kerala and performed creditably in Telangana and Karnataka. With the NDA securing 290-plus seats, Modi returned to power as the prime minister for a third consecutive term—a feat achieved only by Jawaharlal Nehru some sixty years before.

Preface

In the corporate world, 'disruptive innovation' became a buzzword since Clayton Christensen coined it in the mid-1990s. It was used to describe the phenomenon that causes non-conventional but courageous upheavals in established businesses or power centres by new entrants in the market. With the advent, rise and prominence of tech startups in particular, this phenomenon has never been out of conversation. According to Christensen, disruptive innovation happens when a smaller, non-threatening, ground-up company challenges an established business.

The challenger enters the market initially at a small level, targeting a market segment that has remained neglected, or even rejected, by the incumbent. The incumbent does not see the threat because it is focused on its traditional, more profitable segment. The new entrant, meanwhile, innovates and eventually successfully wins over the mainstream customer of the incumbent business.

Similar disruptions can happen in other areas of activity as well. And there are convincing parallels that can be drawn between business, military and political worlds, for instance, when an individual challenges a traditional power structure with out-of-the-box ideas and solutions. We need to apply the business disruptor analogy to Narendra Modi's rise in politics—first as the chief minister of Gujarat and then as the country's prime minister—to understand his success.

PM Modi began his career at the lower rungs of the RSS and went on to work at the organisational levels of the BJP. He then moved into state and national organisations of the party, ultimately becoming the chief minister of Gujarat and later the prime minister of India. Modi's story is a fine example of positive disruption. It is a tale of grit, passion, service, sacrifice, dedication and discipline, interspersed across the socio-religio-political history of Bharat.

Through the 1990s and the 2000s, Modi's rise to a national stature seemed remote. Years later, the BJP's tally in the 2014 Lok Sabha elections was an achievement that not many had dreamed of. But both happened on the strength of fresh ideas, new campaign strategies and their creative implementation helmed by that one man. Modi worked to ensure that his vision of India reached the masses, who eventually voted in his favour in large numbers.

*

Ten years have passed, during which PM Modi has not been out of the news at any time. There is always some pathbreaking announcement or intervention related to one issue or the other. His commitment and drive to serve the people have not wavered since. He takes no leaves and does not let his colleagues to lose focus. It is said that change comes from the top; PM Modi displays exactly how it happens. Everything that has happened in India—revamp of internal security and safer borders, wider and better roads, and so much more—has been rightly credited to PM Modi's leadership. He has brought big changes (for instance, removal of Article 370) and also process reforms that have escaped larger public attention. Every member of his government and party knows that one would have to be reasonably prepared to stand their ground. Further, his impact is not only felt on the recent development story of India but also on the civilizational aspect of our history. What else would the construction of the Ram Mandir or the awakening of the civilizational consciousness of the people be about?

There is perhaps no aspect of our lives that Modi has not touched. This makes me reflect on a private dinner I had in Delhi's Nizamuddin East in early 2024. In attendance were a set of highly accomplished septuagenarians, including hoteliers, diplomats, royalty, bureaucrats, businessmen and politicians. Many of them had been witness to the Congress days. Uncomfortable with and unused to meaningful shakeups, many were ready to crib about the India of today. I, on the other hand, was defending the incumbent prime minister. The conversation ranged from religion to working style to the impression of India across the world and fresh confidence amongst Indians here and abroad. Interestingly, by the end of the supper, everyone was able to reflect on at least two reasons why they would vote for Modi and would like to see him back as the prime minister of India. Everyone agreed that he was good for India and that he was returning to power, no matter what the Opposition might say.

The Disruptor-in-Chief

PM Modi has reshaped so many aspects of our politics and governance that reams can be written about them. While fixing the wrongs is one part, he is also setting the agenda for the future. When he announced the Panch Pran from the ramparts of the Red Fort, he was exhorting the youth of India and setting them on a path to 2047. It's not a shallow promise. Instead, he is setting out a vision much like the great visionaries of Bharat to work towards a developed country although many readers of this book may not be in their prime to witness the changes when they happen.

This book, however, does not detail all the disruptions. That would be a gigantic task. Perhaps, an institutional study could be commissioned for it. Instead, the book takes a look at different themes that are commonly seen today and, perhaps, taken for granted. These themes tell the back story of the disruptive methods PM Modi generated to make the changes happen. For instance, never before has sports received support from the top leadership. Similarly, cleanliness and hygiene have been given the priority they deserve for the first time in decades after Mahatma Gandhi gave a clarion call.

I also discuss the rising reputation of the Indian passport and the confidence of our diaspora. Our foreign policy is now India-centric, and we have stopped pandering to global powers. The book also discusses the dramatic changes in the health sector, where India is increasingly becoming an example of low-cost, quality medical care. Then, of course, there is a chapter on how new-age writing is shaping the discourse of the nation.

Why do I believe that PM Modi is the disrupter-in-chief, who has helped India break from its self-imposed shackles and given Indians a vision for the future and the requisite confidence to turn dreams into reality? When he first assumed the prime ministership in 2014, he came with the reputation of being an 'outsider'. Although, as chief minister he had regular interactions with the central government and the central power structure, he never really identified himself with the ecosystem. Unlike several of his predecessors, he did not have the experience of having worked within the system.

To an extent, he had strong reservations with the system, which he felt had not adequately delivered for the people.

The 'outsider' prime minister then set out to change things. In the process he ruffled many feathers, and people who had entrenched interests in the system felt threatened. He scrapped some institutions (the Planning Commission, for example), created new ones that would reflect the needs of the present (NITI Aayog) and spoke a language that was alien to those who had been brought up—and had flourished—in the old ecosystem. The team that he headed (even though it comprised some old-timers) reflected his new thinking and worked accordingly. More importantly, the bureaucracy, never comfortable with changes, also fell in line.

The policies and programmes announced and implemented over the last decade had a stamp of PM Modi's novel approach. They stretch across many sectors—from education and health to infrastructure and environment to social welfare schemes and digital payments to a revival of the country's civilizational and cultural legacies. PM Modi, however, credits the people for the success of his disruptive methods. He said, 'The title of disruptor-in-chief is not for Modi but 1.25 billon people of this country.'[1]

In many ways that it is true; it is the support and cooperation of the people that has made his unique methods of governance a success.

1

The Modi Phenomenon: Before and After

The dawn of the twenty-first century ushered in a new political ecosystem for India with Atal Bihari Vajpayee as prime minister. Under his leadership, India, that is Bharat, began to slowly but surely leave behind the vestiges of a socialist economy. His policies gave a huge impetus to the unprecedented wave of economic liberalization that had been previously initiated by the P.V. Narasimha Rao government.

From information technology to infrastructure to the export policy and more, India began to take huge strides in almost all sectors. However, it was Vajpayee's bold stance on national security that showed the tough side of the 'poet' prime minister. I would say that it did not fail to impress youngsters like me, who would read and learn about a rather meek India that always invariably folded up under veiled threats or cajoling from the superpowers, friendly or otherwise.

Vajpayee, notwithstanding the threat of economic sanctions by the United States (US) and others who formed the larger 'Amerisphere', gave the green signal for the Pokhran tests, thus firmly establishing India in the league of nuclear powers. That iconic picture of scientist A.P.J. Abdul Kalam—who would go on to become the president of India—along with

Vajpayee, remains entrenched in our minds for posterity. It shows that with resilience and self-belief, there is nothing that a nation cannot achieve, and indigenously too.

It was Vajpayee's policy on Pakistan that elicited widespread attention, not just within the country but also abroad. The sole focus of our foreign policy was to counteract the erratic aggressor-neighbour, who chose to foment terrorism in India for its own domestic political gains. After the bilateral summit in Lahore, which everyone hailed as a breakthrough moment in India–Pakistan relations, and in which many saw a real glimmer of hope for the establishment of peace and goodwill between the two countries, Kargil happened. As a consequence, Vajpayee's Pakistan policy was dissected even more minutely, with some commentators pronouncing it a colossal failure.

The Vajpayee era resulted in some political stability, which, in turn, provided a sense of purpose and direction that India had to take. The country witnessed all-round growth and development in various sectors: financial, social, infrastructure, foreign affairs, etc. The Rao government had brought an economic revolution, but it was during Vajpayee's tenure as prime minister that the country witnessed a larger holistic progress.

Despite these achievements and much to the surprise of many, the 2004 elections threw up an unexpected result: the voters rejected Vajpayee's government, and a new Congress-led dispensation came into place. The reasons are many, and it is not the mandate of this book to go into those details.

Vajpayee is today fondly remembered through the various initiatives named after him. However, the most relevant would be the 'Good Governance' Day that Prime Minister

Modi announced to mark Vajpayee's birth anniversary. This indeed is an appropriate tribute to the man who believed in welfarism and yet stood for principled governance coupled with fiscal prudence. Reams have already been written about Vajpayee. Since the primary focus of this work is not Vajpayee, it would be suffice here to say that Vajpayee's standing in modern Indian political history is among the tallest leaders that ever lived.

An understanding of the Vajpayee era is critical because it was in those years that the protagonist of our story, Narendra Damodardas Modi, entered public and political space. It was under Vajpayee's patronage that Modi got his wings. Besides, to appreciate Modi's rise, it is important to get a sense of his background and context. This, in turn, requires an understanding of the Bharatiya Janata Party (BJP) and its rise from humble beginnings to emerging as arguably the world's largest political party.

And so, before we move on to Modi, it is necessary to understand how the BJP came into existence because that is a story in itself. It is the story of a party that rose on not just the talent of its leaders but also on the nationalist causes it espoused and the democratic manner of its functioning.

History of the BJP

The Bharatiya Jana Sangh (BJS), also popularly known as Jana Sangh, was formed on 21 October 1951, at Raghomal Girls High School, Delhi, with Dr Syama Prasad Mookerjee as its first president. When the Jana Sangh first contested the general elections in 1951–1952, the party faced a huge disappointment despite putting in great efforts; it won just three seats. Throughout its campaign, the BJS forcefully articulated and promoted nationalist ideals in post-Independence India.

The ideological foundations of the Jana Sangh were based on the principles of Hindutva, which sought to uphold and promote the cultural and national identity of the Hindus who comprised an overwhelming majority of the population. The party believed in the idea of a unified and culturally vibrant India that drew inspiration from its ancient heritage. The BJS emphasized the protection of the rights and interests of the Hindu community, particularly in the context of the diverse and pluralistic Indian society, but without considering others as second-class citizens. The party also advocated the abolition of the special status granted to Jammu and Kashmir (J&K), a cause that gained prominence with Syama Prasad Mookerjee's opposition to the then-prevailing permit system in the state. Mookerjee's decision to resign from the Nehru cabinet in protest against the failure of the Indian government to take effective measure in ensuring that the minority Hindus in Pakistan were safe and secure resulted in another important political development: the formation of the Bharatiya Jana Sangh. Mookerjee's death in 1953 (while in custody in J&K) under mysterious circumstances not only raised the party's profile but also popularized the party's nationalistic stand in J&K.

For the Jana Sangh and the BJP later on, therefore, both the issues of J&K and the minorities in Pakistan became the focal points of attention.

While the BJS struggled in its early years to get electoral support, it continued to actively participate, with all the strength it could muster, in national and state elections. The commitment bore fruit when it began to gradually expand its footprint. Although the 1950s turned out to be a disappointment for the party in electoral terms, the decade was not altogether without achievement. The Jana Sangh took up a number of causes that resonated with the people and fetched the party much-needed traction.

While Kashmir remained an important focus for the BJS, the party also launched a movement for the liberation of Goa in 1954 from Portuguese rule. In 1958, it spearheaded the Berubari mass movement, which was launched to protest against the transfer of Berubari from West Bengal to East Pakistan in the east, as per the Radcliffe Award. These mass campaigns seem to resonate with the people at large because the next elections the Jana Sangh fought in 1962 saw the party winning fourteen seats; this tally went up to thirty-five in the 1967 elections.

However, it was only in 1975 that the party emerged as a real force to be reckoned with. The political landscape was going through a churn when Prime Minister Indira Gandhi imposed the Emergency. The BJS, along with other opposition parties, actively opposed the brazen suppression of democracy and the curtailment of civil liberties. This period of resistance against authoritarianism saw the emergence of a united Opposition against the Congress government, an Opposition in which the Jana Sangh was a major player.

In 1977, following the lifting of Emergency, several opposition parties, including the Jana Sangh, came together to form the Janata Party. The Janata Party went on to win the general elections of 1977, leading to the formation of the first non-Congress government at the Centre.

Unfortunately, the Janata Party, which was an umbrella organization under which a number of parties had gathered, faced serious internal strife. When the situation turned from bad to worse, the Janata Party disintegrated, leading to the reorganization of political forces. Writes Kingshuk Nag,

> A month earlier in April 1979, Raj Narain, the man whose election petition had resulted in the high court order unseating Indira Gandhi, had demanded that the Janata Party officially break all ties with the RSS. Jana Sangh elements gathered support from the hundred MPs of the Janata Party and demanded the expulsion of Raj Narain, who was the incumbent health minister from the Janata Party. Raj Narain had also contested against Indira Gandhi in the 1977 Lok Sabha polls and defeated her. The MPs further demanded the expulsion of UP Chief Minister Banarasi Das who led a Janata Party government but without a single minister from the erstwhile Jana Sangh. Banarasi Das had replaced Ram Naresh Yadav who had to quit after losing his majority in the legislature party after he had sacked all ministers who had Jana Sangh origins.
>
> Similarly, in Haryana, Devi Lal had to quit after sacking ministers of Jana Sangh origin from his government. In Bihar, Chief Minister Karpoori Thakur lost his confidence vote, a move that was engineered by legislators with Jana Sangh origins.[1]

The end arrived when Raj Narain left the Janata Party and formed a breakaway group, the Janata Party (Secular). Soon enough, Morarji Desai resigned who was succeeded by Charan Singh. The experiment had failed. Former Jana Sangh members quit and formed a new political party in 1980, which was named the Bharatiya Janata Party. The BJP represented a continuation of the Jana Sangh's legacy. Vajpayee was elected as the founding president of the BJP from 1980 to 1986. The new party geared up for new conquests.

However, the assassination of Prime Minister Indira Gandhi in 1984 changed the ground situation. In the elections that followed the tragic event, the pro-Congress sympathy wave swept the BJP aside; it could win only two seats in the Lok Sabha. The party had to start from near zero to make a mark on the Indian political scene. It was around this time, in 1986, that L.K. Advani took on the reigns of the party (1986–1990). It was the period when Rajiv Gandhi was the prime minister, and the corruption scandal relating to the purchase of Bofors guns erupted in the public domain. The BJP seized the opportunity. Subsequently, the party significantly improved its performance in the 1989 elections. It won eighty-five seats and supported the V.P. Singh-led Janata Dal government at the Centre. The Ayodhya movement was then in its nascent stages, with pro-temple leaders across India making a pitch for a Ram temple at Ayodhya. The theme was played out in every public meeting and gathering.

But it was only in September 1990 that the movement grabbed the national eyeball when Advani launched his historic Rath Yatra from Somnath to unite Indians, particularly Hindus, for the cause of the Ram Mandir. Many credit the idea of the yatras to galvanize votes for Narendra Modi, who was then a worker in the BJP Gujarat organization. He had joined the party organization in Gujarat and energized the cadre. Meanwhile, the BJP withdrew its support to the government. After the Janata Dal government fell and fresh elections were held in 1991, the BJP secured 120 seats. This was also the time when Murli Manohar Joshi became the BJP president; he served in that position until 1993, after which Advani took over the reins again.

It was in the 1990s that the BJP really grew rapidly across India. While it was strong in the northern belt, it also began to be talked of in the south. In the 1996 election, it emerged as the single largest party in the Lok Sabha but fell short of a simple majority. Vajpayee briefly served as the prime minister, leading a coalition government that lasted only thirteen days. In 1999, the BJP-led National Democratic Alliance (NDA) formed a coalition government, with Vajpayee as the prime minister again. The government completed its full term in 2004.

While building over decades of work of former leaders; the BJP, under the leadership of stalwarts such as Atal Bihari Vajpayee and Narendra Modi, has continued to shape India's political landscape. It has emphasized economic reforms, national security, and social issues, while also maintaining its commitment to Hindutva. It is thence fair to say that the journey from the BJS to the BJP reflects the evolution of right-wing politics in India, making it a crucial chapter in the country's political history. The two decades before Vajpayees' prime ministership give great insights into political organization building and the importance of national narratives in galvanizing voters around a cause.

Vajpayee's Role

Atal Bihari Vajpayee's leadership was characterized by charisma, diplomacy, inclusivity, and a commitment to national development. His ability to navigate through intriguing political scenarios and leave a lasting impact on Indian politics has secured him a prominent place in the nation's history. Vajpayee's leadership style is often cited as an example of statesmanship and effective governance in a diverse and complex political environment. Besides being a consummate political leader, Vajpayee was a renowned poet too. His poetry reflected a deep connection with Indian culture and society. This cultural connection resonated with the public and contributed to his popularity. A major contributing factor to his popularity as a speaker was his excellent oratorical skills; in public meetings and in the Parliament, his speeches, punctuated by dramatic pauses, made him a rage.

Vajpayee played a pivotal role in not only shaping the BJP and its fortunes but was also a central figure in developing the nation's political landscape. His leadership style and governance have been subjects of analysis, admiration, and, yes, debate too. While, in hindsight, many commentators now praise his style of functioning, back in the day, when he was just a BJP worker, he was often accused of the same Hindutva policies that Modi was targeted with later.

Vajpayee's initiation into politics was a slow and steady process. His early years saw him take a keen interest in journalism and build a strong foundation of ideological principles. He began as a young student in politics and became one of India's most respected leaders, demonstrating his resilience, political acumen, and commitment to the nation.

Vajpayee was born in Gwalior on 25 December 1924. His father, Krishna Bihari Vajpayee, was a schoolteacher, and his mother, Krishna Devi, was a homemaker. Vajpayee completed his early education in Gwalior and pursued his undergraduate studies at Victoria College (now Laxmi Bai College) in Gwalior; he later graduated with a master's degree in political science from DAV College in Kanpur. He joined the Rashtriya Swayamsevak Sangh (RSS) during his student days, marking the beginning of his association with the organization that would significantly influence his political ideology and also influence the party itself.

Vajpayee began his career as a journalist, working for newspapers and magazines such as *Rashtradharma* and *Panchjanya*, where he contributed articles on political and social issues. His entry into mainstream politics began when he joined the Jana Sangh, in 1951. He became a prominent member of the Jana Sangh and was elected as a member of Parliament (MP) for the first time in 1957.

During Emergency, Vajpayee was arrested, and he spent several months in prison during this period. Later, as prime minister, Vajpayee demonstrated bold leadership by ordering nuclear tests in Pokhran in 1998, making India a declared nuclear weapons state. He pursued a pragmatic and balanced foreign policy, fostering better relations with both Western and neighbouring countries.

Post his prime ministerial tenure, Vajpayee quit active politics and withdrew from public life due to health reasons. He passed away on 16 August 2018, leaving behind a legacy of statesmanship, sensitivity in governance, and political leadership that Narendra Modi epitomizes—the same worker whom Vajpayee had himself mentored. As it turns out, not only was Vajpayee right about Modi, but he also lived to see India in safe hands before he breathed his last.

So, what was the Modi–Vajpayee equation like? How did Modi come to be with the RSS, and how did a regular Swayamsevak go on to become one of the most powerful leaders in the world? Let's rewind to the days of Swayamsevak Modi and his journey to the centre stage of national politics.

Modi's Early Days

Vadnagar in Gujarat was—and, in many ways, still is—a quintessential Indian small town. It is not big, is laid-back, and is home to people from various castes. To father Damodardas and mother Hiraba, he was the third child in a family that traced its roots to Rajasthan and belonged to an extremely backward Ghanchi (Teli) caste (oil-pressing caste). Growing up in a small house, a young Modi was accustomed to a life lived with little means, including fetching water from a well, conducting all household activities with a kerosene lamp for light, and using a nearby lake for daily ablutions. His was a poor family, for whom making both ends meet daily was the chief preoccupation.

Against this backdrop, it becomes easier to understand why Modi, as a politician, gives so much importance to the construction of toilets and the supply of drinking water and electricity. As a child, or while growing up, he did not have the comforts that come with power and privilege. Decades later, as prime minister, when he had both privilege and power, he did not forget his past and ensured that what he missed and what was so essential to a life of dignity was made available to the millions of common citizens of the country.

Modi got attracted to the RSS early on in his life, and he began attending the shakha when he was in Class V.[2] However, his formal introduction into the RSS happened in 1972 in Ahmedabad. Vadnagar was failing to fulfill his aspirations and young Modi moved to Ahmedabad, where he worked at the canteen of his uncle Babubhai at the bus stand of the state transport office. As fate would have it, Modi met Ambalal Koshti here, who was then general secretary of Kankariya ward, Jana Sangh. Modi also befriended other RSS leaders there. Here, he also met his guide and mentor, Laxmanrao Inamdar, whom everyone called Vakil Saheb; it was Imamdar who formally got Modi into the RSS.[3] Vakil Saheb's contribution is very large in the life of Modi, and he helped Modi in his political career as well.

As a child, there was a quiet stubbornness about Modi, which is evident in the way he resisted his family on the subject of marriage. He was just seventeen and did not want to get married. He left home to embark on a journey to the Himalayas or rather to do Bharat Darshan. What today's generation calls 'finding oneself' is what Modi did years ago! He took his parents into confidence about this decision, and while they were naturally aghast, and his mother especially distraught, they did not come in the way of his resolve.

It is perhaps right to argue that to achieve goals that a higher state of mind dictates, for which both unwavering commitment and clarity are needed, one has to leave many things behind. Maybe, that is why the young Narendra left Ahmednagar and started on his exploratory journey. There are many tales about where he went and what he did. But only key elements are known or understood. Modi travelled through the Himalayas and did sadhana, met people from all quarters of life, and understood the country like few others ever would. And all this at the young age of eighteen. 'Not all who wander are lost,' they say. That is what happened to the young Modi. Just out of school, he learnt more about the country, its people, and culture through his journeys.

During this time, Modi was also inspired by the high ideals of Swami Vivekananda. Swamiji was a force of nature and had an early impact on Modi's life. It was only natural that during his self-discovery that the young Narendra would make his way to Belur Math in West Bengal in early 1968. There is an interesting anecdote from those early days.

In 1966 Swami Athamasthananda went to Rajkot, Gujarat, to head the city Ramkrishna Mission (RKM) ashram. Modi reached his doorstep to take refuge. By this time, Modi had already spent some time wandering and was wanting to train himself for a spiritual life. Modi told Swamiji that he wanted to be a monk. However, Modi was told that sanyas was not for him. Even more, the Rajkot ashram could confere monkship. Thereafter, armed with a letter to then president of RKM, Swami Madhavanada, Modi reached Belur. Here also Modi's plea was turned down. Modi returned to Rajkot and learnt more from Swami Atmasthananda[4] before joining RSS and politics.[5]

It is said that after being rejected from Belur, Modi also went to RKM's centre in Almora, the Advaita Ashram. Modi had no option but to head back to the RKM in Rajkot. It was here that Swami Atmasthanandji Maharaj explained to him that he was not suited for the life of a monk and that his destiny lay elsewhere. From this point on, Narendra Modi's life took a turn—and how![6]

Reconnecting with the RSS

With his attempts at monkhood having failed, Modi made his way back to Gujarat and began exploring his life ahead. However, the learnings and understanding of the country he had picked up during his travel began nudging him in a certain direction—a direction that would pick up pace quicker than anyone, including him, had imagined. In fact, looking back, it feels like so much happened in his life and so quickly that one has to slow down to really get a sense of what was happening, much like how one would slow down a video on YouTube to watch key scenes. At that juncture, Modi was sort of reintroduced to the RSS. It could be defined as a critical inflection point in his life. He was first introduced to the RSS at the tender age of eight, and now, almost a decade later, he was back in its fold.

In Gujarat, Modi began his early work in the RSS at the Hedgewar Bhawan. It was a critical juncture in Indian politics. Even as the Gandhi–Nehru family-led Congress ruled the country through all its wits and charms, the RSS worked distant from the limelight in the nooks and corners, where people lived far from the glamour of 'art and culture' of Lutyens' zone. Modi learnt some early and important lessons in the organization, and those learnings would influence him in the years to come and have a bearing on his performance as prime minister.

The state was recovering from the horrific 1969 communal riots that had ravaged Gujarat, and Modi worked closely with his mentor and guide, Vakil Saheb. At the end of eighteen months, he was rewarded with the position of pracharak in the RSS. His organizational skills were being noticed by senior functionaries of the RSS and the Jana Sangh. As time passed, Modi was given more and more work, and he revelled in the additional responsibilities. As a swayamsevak, Modi was involved in many initiatives of the Sangh.

Among other things, he was closely associated with the campaign to expand the network of the organization, spreading its message to the ground and ensuring that people understood the plans, initiatives, and thoughts of the RSS. This was also the time when the Congress party, or more precisely, the Nehru–Gandhi clan, ruled the Indian political scene, and Emergency came into force. One of the first acts of the RSS when this happened was to establish a coordinating committee for a resistance movement called the Gujarat Lok Sangharsh Samiti; Modi was appointed its general secretary.

The appointment during Emergency would prove to be a pivotal point in Modi's rise in the political arena. He was only twenty-five, but years of organizational experience at the Hedgewar Bhawan had taught him all that he needed in people management and more. As he carried out underground activities to resist Emergency, Gujarat stood out like a sore thumb for Indira Gandhi. From sending out the truth of Emergency to foreign media in a clandestine manner to disguising himself to evade arrest by the authorities, Modi was doing all that it took to bring to light the high-handedness of this undemocratic imposition. It was during this time that he met the fiery socialist trade union leader, George Fernandes.

In 1978, Modi was made vibhag pracharak and within two years, promoted to sambhag pracharak. It was also during this phase that Modi contributed to relief and rescue efforts in the aftermath of the Morbi-Machhu Dam disaster. Notably, Modi also wrote the official RSS account of the Emergency period in Gujarat.[7]

However, after the Emergency was over, the non-Congress governments that followed did not have much life, and soon enough, Modi watched from the sidelines how this historic opportunity to make use of the change in power and course correction was lost. It was a lesson that he internalized.

BJP and the 1980s

The 1980s, like the previous decade, was also a politically tumultuous period. After the decline of the Janata Party, the Congress was back in power with Indira Gandhi as the prime minister. Many state governments were toppled soon after she took office. Some escaped; Haryana was one of them, thanks to some smart manoeuvring by then Chief Minister Bhajan Lal. The national government was caught in a web of many contentious issues, including the Khalistan movement. Indira Gandhi ordered the Indian Army to flush out Khalistan activists holed up in the Golden Temple at Amritsar in what was named Operation Bluestar. A few months later, she was assassinated, and her son, Rajiv Gandhi, took office. The elections that followed decimated the entire Opposition, and the BJP was reduced to rubble. But, following some dramatic developments, Rajiv Gandhi lost the next election, and he had to bow out. Multiple scandals had scarred his government. A few years later, he too was assassinated.

A few years ago, after the electoral debacle, the BJS had reinvented itself to form the BJP. Under the leadership of Atal Bihari Vajpayee, Lal Krishna Advani, and leaders of the stature of Murli Manohar Joshi, the BJP began to spread itself. But the media and intellectuals argued that the BJP was essentially a Brahmin–Baniya party, with limited appeal. With time, however, that perception changed, as the party made massive outreaches to other castes and communities. Today, the prime minister is from the Other Backward Class (OBC), and the Modi-led government has given representation to OBCs, Scheduled Castes (SCs), and Scheduled Tribes (STs). In fact, a bulk of the Modi government's support base comprises the OBCs, SCs, and STs.

Modi would soon make his entry into the political arena, writes Kishor Makwana: 'In 1986, Narendra Modi was transferred from the Rashtriya Swayamsevak Sangh to the Bharatiya Janata Party. (*The transfer was not complete, perhaps.)* He became the general secretary of the state organisation.'[8] He took upon himself the task of firmly expanding the scope of the party. He prepared a database to enroll members of the party, as well as constitute booth, area, district, and state committees, and this effort led to a state-level data bank. This comprised extensive and detailed information of all workers in Gujarat. Hardworking and loyal people from all fields of life were brought into politics in a bid to improve upon the image of politics. It helped to bring the youth into politics, especially because of the efforts in this field. During 1985–86, the administration had decided not to take out the historical Rath Yatra in Ahmedabad due to communal riots, but Modi used his insight and strategy to befool the police and take it out.

The entire responsibility regarding election strategy, planning, operation, and propaganda was borne by Modi. At that time, he gave the slogan: '*Ab to bas Bhajpa—ek mauka Bhajpa ko*' (The BJP this time—one opportunity to the BJP.) This slogan struck the minds of people quite rapidly.[9]

Modi's impact on organizational structure and unconventional modes of party expansion began showing results. The thirty-six-year-old Modi was given charge of the Ahmedabad municipal corporation elections. Given his organizational experience, this was Modi's trial by fire for a political cause. With the help of his methodical approach, the party crossed the halfway mark, and the Congress, taken by surprise, had reasons to be worried.[10]

During this period, the sectarian KHAM (Koli Kshatriya, Harijan, Adivasi, and Muslim) politics, the overturning of the Shah Bano case, and the opening of the Babri mosque for Shila Nyas kept the country and state on edge. It was as if India was simmering with angst and rage, but matters had not yet reached the boiling point. Soon after the AMC elections, Modi decided to take out a series of rallies all over Gujarat, beginning with Nyay Yatra. After studying the impact of the droughts of 1985, 1986, and 1987, Modi started this rally for justice, aimed at making people aware of their entitlements. The yatra was meted with grand support and welcome.[11]

In June 1989, Modi organized the Lok Shakti Yatra from the temple of Shakti at Ambaji.

> In the Lok Sabha election of 1989, the BJP allied with the Janata Dal at the last moment, agreeing to contest twelve seats, vacating the rest fourteen for V.P. Singh's party. Given the anti-Congress mood after the Bofors scandal, V.P. Singh had emerged as a charismatic leader and became the prime minister, but in Gujarat his party won eleven out of fourteen seats, whereas the BJP won all the twelve seats it had contested. (The Congress was reduced to three seats.) The BJP thus emerged as the number one party—all efforts over the years had borne fruit.[12]

Even more, in the Gujarat Assembly elections in March 1990, BJP won 67 seats.[13]

Later, in September 1990, in the final weeks of V.P. Singh's administration, when the Somnath to Ayodhya yatra set off from Gujarat, Modi's experience in organizational matters made the Gujarat leg of the journey a huge success; he followed the yatra as far as Mumbai. Adds Singh,

> There is no denying the fact that the Gujarat leg of the Rath Yatra had set the pace for the rest of India. At the same time, Gujarat managed to reap maximum political benefit from the exercise, which subsumed caste cleavages and coalesced Hindu society in one identity for the first time. Significantly, the Sangh Parivar's organizational network was at the vanguard of this social cohesion, which subsequently turned into a great political advantage.[14]

The third significant yatra was about a year after the Somnath–Ayodhya one. Here he was not only looking after the Gujarat leg but was given the charge of coordination for the full route.[15] This forty-seven-day Ekta Yatra, with the new BJP national president,

Murli Manohar Joshi, began in December 1991 at the southern tip of the country, Kanyakumari in Tamil Nadu, and ended with Modi and his associates hoisting the national flag in Srinagar, Kashmir, in the new year. What happened is no mean feat. While addressing a rally in Jammu on the 24th, he said, '*Lal Chowk mein poster lagaye, deewaaron pe likha hai, jisne apni maa ka doodh piya haivo Srinagar ke lal chowk pe aayein; aakarke Baharat ka tiranga feraayein. Aur agar vo zinda waapis jayega to atankwaadi use inaam denge.*'[16]

He retorted, '*26 January ko ... Lal Chowk mein faisla ho jayega kisne apni Maa ka doodh piya hai.*'[17]

On 26 January, at 11 a.m., Modi with Joshi and others hoisted the tricolour in Srinagar. Famously, this was the trip on which Modi refused to put on the body armour he was advised to wear or take a dedicated security entourage—a successful piece of theatrics that raised awareness of the need to stand against terrorism fearlessly.[18]

Politics in Gujarat was going through a churn in the early 1990s. Modi was marginalized by S.S. Vaghela but that did not deter him or his work. It is also said that he temporarily withdrew from active politics as the mood of the country was fraught with communal violence and more.[19] Instead, he continued to focus on party work and on the school he was helping to build in the memory of his mentor, Vakil Saheb. The said school is Sanskardham, a 125-acre complex that opened in June 1992 and housed Laxman Gyanpith Secondary School.

The years were full of turmoil laden with Rajiv Gandhi's assassination, communal violence, terrorism, and the demolition of Babri Masjid. Alongside this, the liberalization reforms gave a fresh lease of life to the Indian economy.

Modi's performance as a party organizer was rewarded in 1990 when he was named as one of the seventeen members of the BJP's National Election Committee, a move that formally recognized his success in Gujarat.[20] The promotion was vital insofar as it took Modi's realm of operations beyond the borders of Gujarat for the first time since he had joined the BJP.

However, Gujarat's politics and leadership were divided on authority. Modi was caught in the midst of the turmoil. Factionalism within the BJP was hampering his progress. And, effectively Modi was on his first *vanvas*. However, on the insistence of Advani, he was sent back to work for the Assembly elections of 1995.

The results were remarkable. Modi's groundwork reaped results when the BJP won a two-thirds majority. However, as the next chain of events unfolded, Modi was compelled to quit, as documented in the famous letter from September 1995: '[I]t is better that I give this party to you and I am leaving.' But Advani stepped in and Modi was appointed National Secretary of the party in November 1995. Modi moved out of Gujarat which could well be treated as his *vanvas*. The prevailing political rivalries in the state had made it difficult for him to perform, and it was considered that Modi's organizational skills should be used in other parts of the country for the party's benefit. In 1996, Modi was put in charge of organizing the BJP in Haryana, Himachal Pradesh, Chandigarh, Punjab, and J&K. He fondly remembers these days for he travelled much, learnt much, and worked with many senior leaders.

Modi, in those days, used to live close to my ancestral home in Sector 7, Panchkula. It was a delightful surprise to learn about the house he had rented and how the landlord Mahabir ji and his family extended help to him during those years. It is noteworthy that when he became prime minister,

Modi called the family for his oath-taking ceremony. In fact, women of the family tied Rakhi on the prime minister's wrist. Modi does not forget the people who stood by him when he went through the tribulations of life.

Modi, the Observer in Delhi

From Haryana, Modi was moved to Delhi, as General Secretary (Organisation) for the BJP. It is here that he saw the workings of national politics from close quarters. As Modi's profile and scope of work kept expanding, he was also the silent observer, watching the politics that was shaping India: from Narasimha Rao's five-year tenure (despite heading a minority government) to the first term of Vajpayee, the Kargil War, and the full term of Vajpayee as prime minister.

Post-Babri, the religious fervour that had gripped the nation began to dwindle, and India rode the wave of liberalization in the Rao era, with Manmohan Singh as the finance minister. Hindutva was seemingly slowly relegated to the background. Affluence and economic freedom broadened and softened it until, eventually, Hindutva began to look like a vessel that could hold something more akin to a confident cultural nationalism. It could appeal to the new middle class, which was thoroughly celebrating the demise of the Licence Raj and soaking in the new-found pleasures of a global lifestyle.

These developments transformed the fortunes of the BJP. In an interview that he gave later, Advani pointed out to a journalist how 'a party based on ideology can at the most come to power in a small area. It cannot win the confidence of the entire country—neither the Communist Party nor [could] the Jana Sangh in its original form'.[21] Now, one may agree that this could have been the stance of the BJP or could argue that this was a requirement of politics of the day.

Regardless Modi absorbed all of it from the sidelines. Argues Modi's biographer,

> He [Modi] too knew that India could only be governed from the centre, not the extremes. Hindutva, he shrewdly judged, could initially win votes, but it was development that offered sustained electoral power. He would employ that principle as chief minister of Gujarat within a decade, though the outcome at first was fraught with unintended consequences.[22]

*

While this happened, a BJP government took office in New Delhi under Prime Minister Vajpayee in March 1998. It was India's first NDA government, and it was also the beginning of an era of multiparty coalition governments. By 1999, Modi had also won the confidence of Vajpayee. He was appointed as the national spokesperson of the party in 1999. He also began travelling abroad (as many as forty countries), gaining exposure and learning. He appeared more frequently on TV debates and was present in Kashmir when the Kargil war broke out.[23]

However, Gujarat without Modi was in disarray. Politically, the BJP was losing ground. Then chief minister Keshubhai Patel was losing grip. BJP in Modi's home state of Gujarat was being eaten from within. Assailed by allegations of corruption and nepotism, the BJP government lost its foothold in key municipalities between 1999 and 2001. Was it time for a new leader for Gujarat? Only time would tell. A natural calamity held the clue. And, this time around, none in the BJP Gujarat could pin the blame on Modi.

Modi in Gujarat and UPA in the Centre

In Gujarat, while the BJP was strong, so was Keshubhai, as he had won with a good majority. Therefore, rumours of Modi trying to topple him remained just that—rumours. However, Keshubhai's handling of the 1998 Kandla cyclone, the Ahmedabad floods of 2000, and the catastrophic Kutch earthquake of January 2001 changed the fortunes of Keshubhai and consequently, Modi. While Modi visited his home state on official matters for short periods of time, what was noticeable was the huge support he was drawing from the common Gujarati.

The sequence of disasters and their mishandling had begun to earn Keshubhai the unfortunate nickname of 'Mr. Disaster'. It was, thence, the Bhuj earthquake that changed Gujarat forever in many ways. Fearful of a tepid performance in the upcoming state elections due to the poor management by the state regime of the catastrophe, Modi was sent as a 'caretaker chief minister' and an Advani protégé till the leadership decided on a 'permanent' name. This change, many would argue, was 'long debated and reluctantly taken'[24]. Some accounts suggest that Vajpayee played a critical role in the decision to get Modi in Gujarat. It is said Modi insisted that he remain a worker, but it was Vajpayee who coaxed him to take the offer. In October 2001, Modi was sworn in as the chief minister. He entered the legislature in February 2002 and cemented his position as the leader-supreme in Gujarat.

Vajpayee stayed in office until 2004, following which from 2004 to 2014, the Sonia Gandhi-led United Progressive Alliance (UPA) ruled the country with Manmohan Singh as the prime minister. In these ten years, as economic growth happened on the foundations of land monetization and non-performing assets, people close to the family flourished like never before. Italian cuisine, French arts, German engineering, Turkish design elements, etc., became the symbols of refinement. The Left-leaning academia was charmed into comfy posts and enjoyed a life of equal pomp. 'Copperplate' font was their way of expressing elitism, all of which was thoroughly detached from Bharat. Even more, this charade was built on the political certainty of an evergreen Congressman authority (as had been the case since Independence) and a rather long slew of scams and scandals.

Looking back to those ten years, one can recall a fine economist Sardar who would speak little. Almost servile, if not wholly, to the Congress's first family. From scams in spectrum and coal allocation to those in the Commonwealth Games and housing, the UPA rule disappointed—if not shocked—millions. These scandals exposed rampant corruption, nepotism, and misuse of power at the highest levels of government, tarnishing the image of Indian democracy and eroding public trust. The 2G spectrum scam, arguably one of the most infamous scandals in India's history, unfolded in 2008 during the tenure of A. Raja (from the Dravida Munnetra Kazhagam or DMK), who was then the minister of communications and information technology. The scam involved the arbitrary allocation of 2G spectrum licenses to telecom companies at grossly undervalued prices, causing an estimated loss of ₹76 lakh crore to the exchequer, according to the Comptroller and Auditor General (CAG). The scam highlighted the nexus between politicians, bureaucrats, and corporate entities, with rampant kickbacks and bribery.

The 2010 Commonwealth Games held in Delhi were marred by allegations of widespread corruption and mismanagement. The organizing committee, headed by a Congress leader, Suresh Kalmadi, came under intense scrutiny for irregularities in awarding contracts, inflated prices of goods and services, and substandard infrastructure. The total cost of the games ballooned to over ₹70,000 crore, making it one of the most expensive sporting events in history. Investigations revealed a web of corruption involving politicians, bureaucrats, and contractors, with funds meant for infrastructure development siphoned off through kickbacks and embezzlement.

The coal allocation scam (2004–09; draft report by CAG in 2012) revolved around irregularities in the allocation of coal blocks to private companies for captive use. The CAG estimated the loss to the exchequer due to arbitrary coal block allocations at ₹1.86 lakh crore. The scam exposed the opaque and arbitrary nature of the allocation process, with favouritism and crony capitalism prevailing over the fair competition. The beneficiaries of the coal allocations included some of India's wealthiest industrialists and influential politicians.

The Adarsh Housing Society scam (CAG Report 2011) centred around the illegal construction of a high-rise residential building in Mumbai, meant to provide housing for war widows and veterans. However, it was revealed that the apartments were allocated to politicians, bureaucrats, and military officials at below-market rates through fraudulent means. The scam exposed collusion between government officials, real estate developers, and defence personnel to usurp prime land and flout zoning regulations. Apart from this, there were other such developments that would put to shame many who took pride in being Indians. Corruption was a way of life, and decency in public-political life vanished into thin air. A change was needed! Perhaps, that is why a larger, in some way organic, movement began in the name of India Against Corruption.

Trial by Fire

Modi was observing these developments from close quarters, and even though there were other tall leaders in the party, his working style was unquestionable; he was putting in long hours and strenuous effort for the party. The scams of the UPA era were a sobering reminder of the dangers of unchecked power and the corrosive impact of corruption on democratic institutions. These scandals not only inflicted substantial financial losses on the nation but also eroded public trust in governance and democratic processes.

However, while he was observing this from afar, it was not as if his chief ministership was a bed of roses. In fact, conditions were far from that. It was a gruelling time for Modi from the word go. While he was busy rebuilding Bhuj, which was recovering from the massive earthquake in January 2001, he realized that this was just the beginning of his trial by fire.

Godhra and 2002—these two terms were to haunt him for what would seem forever. The Godhra incident erupted in the aftermath of the burning of the Sabarmati Express train, which was carrying Hindu pilgrims returning from Ayodhya. The incident, in which fifty-nine passengers, mostly Hindu activists, were killed, was attributed to a mob of Muslims. The gruesome nature of the attack and the loss of innocent lives triggered outrage and sparked communal tensions in Gujarat. This led to full-blown riots across the state, characterized by widespread arson, looting, and targeted attacks on both Muslim and Hindu communities. This was shortly after Modi assumed office, and it ended up casting a shadow over his administration and raising questions about his handling of communal tensions.

While allegations over the 'delay' in his controlling the riots were flowing thick and fast, a fact check revealed that he had acted in earnest, and it was, in fact, other Congress-led states that had refused to help by not sending additional security troops. Later, the Supreme Court gave him a clean chit over the incident. The matter should have ended there. However, an entire industry was born out of Godhra, which included the media, NGOs, foreign publications, and human rights organizations. Their main task, it seemed, was to continue spinning a narrative on 'divisive Modi', and to a large extent, they succeeded. Thousands of articles on the subject have ensured that only anti-Modi articles come up in a simple Google search—facts be damned!

But while this flawed narrative was being lapped up across India, in Gujarat, where the anti-Modi impact should have been the most—if one believes the accusations levelled against him as being true—things were different. The state under Modi was flourishing, and voters gave resounding mandates repeatedly. During his time in office, Modi implemented a series of innovative policies and initiatives aimed at driving economic growth, infrastructure development, and social progress in the state. He prioritized economic growth and industrialization, positioning Gujarat as a leading destination for investment and business. Modi's proactive stance on infrastructure development, including roads, ports, and power generation, laid the foundation for Gujarat's economic prosperity. So much so, that the Gujarat Model of Development became national news.

The state's Gross State Domestic Product (GSDP) consistently outpaced the national average, reflecting Gujarat's resilience and competitiveness in the global economy. Modi's focus on inclusive growth ensured that the benefits of development reached all segments of society, including marginalized communities and rural areas. The establishment of ports such as Mundra and Pipavav positioned Gujarat as a maritime hub, catalyzing trade and logistics. Additionally, Modi's emphasis on renewable energy initiatives, such as solar power projects, showcased Gujarat's commitment to sustainable development and environmental conservation. While driving economic growth, Modi also focused on enhancing social welfare and human development indicators in Gujarat. Initiatives like the Kanya Kelavani (Girl Child Education) and Beti Bachao, Beti Padhao campaigns aimed at promoting female education and empowerment yielded positive outcomes. Modi's efforts in healthcare, including the implementation of the Chiranjeevi Yojana for maternal and child healthcare, contributed to improved health outcomes and access to medical facilities, especially in rural areas. His emphasis on skill development and vocational training initiatives enhanced employability and livelihood opportunities for the youth.

Through his vision, determination, and focus on development, Modi propelled Gujarat onto the global stage as a model of economic progress and social transformation. And this was why the state voted him back to power, over and over again, for three consecutive terms. The agenda-jeevis had no clue as to how this was happening. They were under the illusion that Modi could be stopped and that his development agenda would fail to click with the voters. But, in Gujarat, he seemed unstoppable.

Little did the critics know, or maybe they knew but pretended otherwise, that the person who had become a state hero would soon be a hero of Bharat.

Modi-RSS-BJP

Modi's journey shows the deep connection he has with both his parent organizations—the BJP and the RSS. As a foot soldier, he learnt the ropes of not just the organization but also the various issues that were plaguing the nation. Many still do not understand the relationship that the RSS has with the BJP. In fact, it is funny that some casually remark that Modi and the RSS are at loggerheads with each other. There are also times when the media sensationalizes a story, wherein someone would argue that the RSS was not happy with Modi's ways, etc. Not only is this utter nonsense, but it is also ridiculous.

The Sangh and the BJP complete and complement each other. If the BJP is not an extension of the RSS, it is a political arm. The party may not be totally under the control of the RSS, yet there is always RSS representation in the form of the organization secretary of the party. Now, many fail to understand how this relationship works. There is nothing complicated. Imagine it being a large family where everyone is in touch with one another. The patriarch at the top manages every member's request and plea. Like in the case of family members, there might be some conflicts now and then, but everyone is together on the larger cause. These sets of people are, of course, those who have been associated with the party as workers or have worked as a part of the Sangh Parivar in close coordination with the party. This lot understands the ways of the party well enough. Many of the leaders have been cleansed through a dip into the Sangh waters! And, some are lateral entrants. These are those powerful leaders who were previously with the Congress or other parties and, out of political necessity or compelling synergies, have joined the BJP. This group of people, having been trained under their former bosses (which, in most cases, is the Congress), initially perhaps believe that even the BJP works like their previous bosses. They are soon divested of the illusion, and then they either re-adjust or quit.

Until Vajpayee's prime ministership, the Nehru–Gandhi family lived like the royals of our democratic republic. Be it public space or private life, nothing was left untouched by the family. Anyone who had to prosper in the country had to become friends, join the coterie, have access to the eminent group, or bow down to the high lords. Delhi's Lutyens Zone decided what should happen in the country. The media and academia were so well controlled that the agony, pains, disappointments, and tragedies of the middle class and the underprivileged remained unheard or were given token attention at best. In fact, this mindset is one prominent reason why Modi's rise is not accepted by that group of pseudo-elites to this day. This privileged group had made careers and lives under the tutelage of the Congress family.

The ones who gained access to the family had nothing to fear. Be it prime positions, businesses, political power, etc., everything was routed from the gates of the Nehru–Gandhi homes. In fact, to date, some of them are still under the impression that the family will return to the high pedestal, and they will reap the benefits of the long wait. So self-centred are these people that they are ready to overlook every positive change that has happened in the country.

And, for those whose social prestige was determined by how well they pleased the family heirs, the rise of Modi was like a 'slash and burn' event on the plantation they had long cultivated and nurtured.

2

A Trigger of Hope

It was an uncanny choice of venue for a politician from Gujarat, not a familiar figure in the Delhi circuit, to herald his arrival on the national stage. Thus, some eyebrows were raised when Narendra Modi zeroed in on the tony Shri Ram College of Commerce to soft-launch his campaign for the 2014 elections. It was still February of 2013, and for the youth, by virtue of their age, those elections were probably not even on their minds. But seventy-five minutes later, not only did those 2,000 students listen in rapt attention to Modi that day, but many other youngsters across India were also talking of development, infrastructure, politics, and yes, elections!

Modi had indeed carefully picked his venue, his audience, and his talking points. For the youth grappling with the seemingly unending grim news of scams and misgovernance, it was a mesmerizing speech. They hardly expected a politician to speak to them about their key role and their 'new-age power' in the growth and development of India. Calling them 'mouse charmers' who were digitally ruling the world, the then chief minister spoke of Brand India and how the youth of the country could play a critical role in making India globally competitive. The speech, which was telecast live across India, got students talking. Indians in general, and the Opposition in particular, were just getting a sneak peek into the juggernaut that was to follow.

By then, two things had become clear. One, that the nation and its people were fed up with the scams and scandals, the terrible state of internal security, and the country's image abroad, which was in shambles. I witnessed the anti-corruption movement in Delhi, during my graduation days. There was a fair amount of frustration in young and old, alike. Metro trains, buses, autos, etc.—all public spaces were buzzing with conversations around the same. And, two, that the country was looking for a change, and as we approached 2014, Modi was the one political leader making the maximum impact. Such a scenario meant that the space for a clean and strong leader was building up, and the people of India were eager to offer it to the right candidate.

It was as if the audience was waiting for a leader who could speak the language of assertiveness in the country's interests. Terror strikes, masterminded by elements from across the border, had become routine. Little was being done to prevent these attacks or to act against Pakistan, which was openly sponsoring the campaign. In fact, if one observes from 2005 onwards, there were a string of terror attacks across the country. In fact, it would feel like an attack every month. As newspapers, TV channels, and social media took early roots in our lives, they'd all cover these developments. And, Indians would hang their heads subconsciously feeling inferior; a country of over a billion people could not defend itself , let alone muster a counter-attack.

In that scenario, Modi appeared as the most viable alternative, having a proven track record of clean governance, administrative acumen, and, more importantly in the given context, assertive leadership. His track record of handling terror cases and making Gujarat amongst the safest states of the country also appealed to the people of India. Besides, the state's growth rate, manufacturing ability, and robust law and order situation made it an ideal destination for professionals to migrate to and for businesses to establish their operations. While internal politics and conversations were going on within the BJP, Modi was being elevated to bigger roles on the national stage after his assembly victory. But it was only in September 2013 that the BJP announced that Gujarat chief minister Modi would be the the prime minsterial face of the BJP. In the media room packed with reports at the BJP's national headquarters at Ashoka Road, Rajnath Singh, who was then the BJP national president, made the announcement, much to the excitement and anticipation of party workers. The announcement charged the crowd and well-wishers across the world and inspired them to work for one goal, and one goal only—to defeat the Congress in 2014, and to make Modi the prime minister of India.

Innovative Approaches

Soon after it became clear that Modi would be BJP's prime ministerial candidate, the election campaign in India took off in top gear. While Modi had a team assisting him in contesting the elections, alongside the BJP organization, many volunteers also participated in the campaign. Some of them even travelled from abroad to join the march.

Multiple groups emerged who brought forth innovative ideas to spread the message of Modi. One innovative campaign in that phase of 2014 was 'Chai pe Charcha', which emerged as a distinctive feature, blending the love of Indians for a cup of tea along with discussing politics in an informal setting with the optimal use of social media handles by the man himself. Modi was way ahead of his political rivals in the digital space. Far from dissing it as a fad for youngsters, he embraced this new way of communication and used it not just to his advantage but also to his party's.

Chai Pe Charcha was a grassroots approach, rooted in the ethos of simplicity and accessibility. It helped bridge the gap between the political elite and the common man. Modi's team employed innovative digital strategies, including active engagement on platforms such as Twitter (now X) and Facebook, live webcasts of rallies, and interactive mobile apps. This approach allowed Modi to bypass traditional media channels and directly communicate with millions of voters, thereby amplifying his message and mobilizing support.

He also embarked on extensive nationwide campaign tours, crisscrossing the country to rally support for the BJP and himself. His rallies attracted large crowds, and his dynamic oratory skills resonated with audiences across different regions and demographics. These high-profile events not only bolstered Modi's image as a charismatic leader but also helped galvanize support for the BJP's electoral prospects. Remembered a senior journalist who attended some of his key rallies in Haryana: '*Pehli baar humne itni well-organised rallies dekhi thi.*' Recognizing the demographic shifts in India, Modi's campaign made concerted efforts to appeal to young and urban voters. He focused on issues such as job creation, entrepreneurship, and modernization, thus tapping into the aspirations of India's burgeoning urban middle class. Modi's message of economic growth and good governance struck a chord, especially with this demographic slice of the population, which contributed significantly to his electoral success.

Modi leveraged his personal rapport, built over the years, with regional leaders, and negotiated strategic partnerships to broaden the BJP's electoral base. This collaborative approach helped consolidate the anti-incumbency sentiments against the ruling Congress-led UPA and positioned the BJP-led NDA as a viable alternative.

Overall, Modi's election strategy in 2013 prepared the ground for his historic victory in the 2014 general elections. By combining a development-centric agenda with strategic messaging, innovative use of technology, and extensive grassroots campaigning, he succeeded in capturing the imagination of the Indian electorate and ushering in a new era of governance at the national level. The election campaign of the BJP with Modi as its face succeeded due to multiple reasons.

The first was that the NDA was the only alliance to go into the elections with a clear leader. The Congress did everything except go public with an official announcement of Rahul Gandhi as its candidate. The so-called third front wanted voters to vote for different leaders in different states but left the question of prime ministership unanswered. In such a scenario, the people of India only had one face that was projected with conviction, and that too it was a face with a proven track record, which was Modi.

The second reason was that Modi appeared to have the answers to India's economic woes. He had demonstrated his administrative acumen with what he delivered for the people of Gujarat and now promised even better for the whole of India. He promised jobs, investment for businesses, and, importantly, a corruption-free government. He constantly referred to the policy paralysis that had afflicted the last years of the UPA government. Referring to his days as chief minister, which had become his calling card, he pointed out that there wasn't a single accusation of graft against him during his twelve-year tenure in Gujarat; by contrast, the UPA had multiple scams to its name, which had drained the country's resources.

The third reason for the success was Modi's individuality. His charisma, connection with the audience, oratory skills, and grasp of what the audience wanted—all of it ticked the right boxes of what Indians wanted from their prime minister. He knew exactly what to say, where to say what, whom to invoke in which state, and what promises to make to whom. Perhaps, this came from his decades-long training as an RSS pracharak, and, thereafter, as an organization man in the BJP.

People knew why they were voting for Modi—he promised better days for them and a better India for all. No one in the history of independent India's elections had shown such clarity of vision and motivation to take the country to greater heights. He also promised to tackle terrorism with the force it deserved.

The Power of Many

It was a celebratory drive soon after the campaign began. People from Singapore, the US, the UK, Canada, etc., came back to the country in hordes just to put in their work for Modi's election campaign. While it is understandable that people from the same neighbourhood with the same political inclination would get together for gatherings, something more cosmic was evolving organically. Much like how families converge on the arrival of a newborn or when someone from the family begins doing remarkably well on the global stage, Indians all across the world came together in the name of Modi. People would call each other, enquiring if they were doing something for the campaign. This, of course, was quite different from what the party itself was doing. Young and old, men and women, would start campaigns or wear the saffron colour to project how they were voting for the BJP because their prime ministerial candidate was Modi.

It is conveniently said that Indians vote for their caste or community. Even more, they vote for the candidate, unless, of course, it's a wave or an overriding emotion that drives an election campaign. But what happened in 2014 was a tsunami, trashing conventions. In fact, it's a feeling that only those involved in the campaign can remember or recollect. There was overall joy in the air. Optimism about change. Modi was on a whirlwind tour across India. The BJP led an exceptional and clinical political campaign. As fortune tellers got louder, so did many politicians across the country, who left old linkages and jumped ship. The BJP family got bigger. Each passing day, each campaign idea, each slogan, each speech, and each media presence made it clear who was going to become the next prime minister of the country.

Notably, it was not just the regular voters who were being tapped by this remarkable campaign. There were corporates, retired bureaucrats, and business houses that were reached out to. Captain Abhimanyu, the former finance minister of Haryana, remembered in a private conversation at his residence in Delhi: 'The party reached out to a diverse spectrum including business leaders, industry associations, economists, business media representatives, and corporates, etc. They were told about Modi's plan for economic growth and development.' Many business houses were similarly contacted. A well-structured plan for the economic future was also laid out. These deliberations gave more confidence to the industry that is the backbone of Indian economy.

The party's election manifesto for 2014 was crafted with great precision. It reflected a comprehensive vision for governance, encompassing economic growth, national security, social justice, and cultural identity. It resonated with voters across various segments and played a significant role in shaping the party's electoral narrative during the campaign. It was aptly titled 'Election Manifesto—Lok Sabha 2014: Ek Bharat, Shreshtha Bharat' (One India, Supreme India). It outlined the party's vision, policies, and promises for governance if elected to power. A lot of the things promised in that manifesto have been delivered today. A cursory reading tells the story.

Economic development

- Setting up a National e-Market for agricultural produce to ensure fair prices for farmers
- Establishment of agro-based industries and food processing units in rural areas
- Creation of a national optical fibre network to connect all villages and gram panchayats
- Implementation of Goods and Services Tax (GST) to streamline taxation and boost economic growth
- Launching a National River-Linking Project to address water scarcity and promote irrigation

One of the flagship promises of the BJP's manifesto was the implementation of GST to streamline taxation and promote economic integration. The government successfully introduced the GST regime in 2017, replacing a complex web of indirect taxes with a unified tax structure, enhancing tax compliance, and fostering a common market across states. Significant investments were made in sectors such as roads, railways, ports, and airports, with flagship initiatives like the Bharatmala project aimed at improving connectivity and boosting economic growth. The government launched various financial inclusion initiatives, including the Pradhan Mantri Jan Dhan Yojana (PMJDY), to provide banking services to the unbanked population.

Job creation and skill development

- Setting up 100 new cities with world-class infrastructure and facilities
- Launching a National Skill Development Mission to train and empower youth for employment opportunities
- Reviving manufacturing and promoting the Make in India initiative to boost domestic production and exports

Governance reforms

- Establishing a transparent and accountable government through measures such as the Right to Services
- Strengthening local self-government institutions and promoting decentralization of power
- Implementing a National Judicial Commission to ensure judicial accountability and expedite justice delivery

National security

- Enhancing defence capabilities and modernizing the armed forces to safeguard India's sovereignty and territorial integrity
- Strengthening border security through the use of technology and infrastructure
- Implementing a zero-tolerance policy towards terrorism and insurgency, with a focus on intelligence-led operations

The government took proactive measures to strengthen national security and combat terrorism, in line with its manifesto commitments. Initiatives such as surgical strikes underscored the Modi government's resolve to safeguard India's sovereignty and tackle cross-border terrorism effectively. The government initiated defence procurement reforms, streamlined defense acquisitions, and prioritized indigenous defense production through initiatives like Make in India for Defence.

Foreign policy

- Pursuing a proactive and assertive foreign policy to protect India's strategic interests and promote regional stability
- Strengthening ties with neighbouring countries through enhanced economic cooperation, cultural exchanges, and diplomatic engagement
- Diplomatic engagement initiatives such as the Act East Policy and Neighbourhood First Policy underscored India's commitment to fostering cooperation and connectivity in the region.
- Reviving India's role as a leader in regional and global forums, including the United Nations, BRICS, SCO, and G20

The Modi government pursued a proactive neighbourhood policy, strengthening relations with neighbouring countries and promoting regional stability. The BJP government actively engaged with the international community in line with its vision of a strong and assertive India on the global stage. Prime Minister Modi's diplomatic outreach and participation in multilateral forums elevated India's stature and influence in international affairs.

Social justice and inclusion

- Ensuring effective implementation of affirmative action policies for SCs, STs, and other marginalized communities
- Strengthening the National Commission for Women and introducing measures to ensure the safety and empowerment of women
- Promoting inclusive education and healthcare initiatives to bridge socioeconomic disparities

Environment and conservation

- Launching National Mission on Clean Ganga to rejuvenate the river and ensure its ecological sustainability
- Promoting renewable energy sources, such as solar and wind power, to reduce carbon emissions and combat climate change
- Strengthening environmental regulations and enforcement mechanisms to protect biodiversity and natural habitats

Cultural heritage and national identity

- Establishing the National Heritage Mission to preserve and promote India's cultural heritage sites and monuments.
- Promoting traditional arts, crafts, and cultural practices through financial support and promotional initiatives
- Fostering a sense of national pride and identity through education, awareness campaigns, and patriotic initiatives

Overall, the BJP's fulfilment of its manifesto commitments since 2014 has played a pivotal role in shaping India's trajectory towards inclusive growth, development, and global leadership.

Alongside many of these developments, the idea of 'good governance' along the lines of the Gujarat model of development became the catchphrase for the election. People had witnessed how Gujarat became a model state of sorts. They were being encouraged to visit Ahmedabad or become a part of the Vibrant Gujarat Global Summit. If one wanted to invest, Gujarat was touted as a place for *dhando.* Even more, there were many other projects with a long focus and clear vision for the overall development of the region. Take, for instance, the Sabaramati Riverfront project.

Chief Minister Modi took on the task and redeveloped the entire area. The river bed was cleaned and revamped and the areas around it were beautified. There was thus a dramatic change in the riverfront, which now looks beautiful and has become a picnic spot. I think that this riverfront exemplified the transformative impact of visionary leadership, innovative urban planning, and community engagement in revitalizing urban water. The renewed Sabarmati Riverfront has since emerged as a popular destination for tourism, recreation, and cultural activities. The development of riverfront promenades, event spaces, and public amenities attracted visitors from across Gujarat and beyond, contributing to the local economy and promoting tourism-related businesses.

As the popularity of Modi and his schemes soared, people would remark, 'Load shedding? *Gujarat mein 24x7 bijli aur paani*—no matter where you live. Our kids haven't heard of loadshedding at all! It used to happen but in the past.'

And these happy conversations happened even as the unfolding coal block allocation scam had left the country stupefied. Here, we had a government in Gujarat that had the makings of a potential power block. And, here we had a chief minister who was ensuring that the last citizen of his state had access to basic facilities. Stories abounded of Gujarat's government schools, which were clean and had modern education and 24x7 power and water supply in every village and district. The professional approach of government servants and the state-conducted business summits were the other talking points ahead of the 2014 elections. People would often say that if a leader can do such wonders for Gujarat, he can repeat the feat for India too.

All these developments were being analyzed by the common man, who juxtaposed them against the systemic problems in other parts of India and the malfunctioning of the union government. The Indian bureaucracy grappled with deep-rooted challenges such as corruption, inefficiency, and a lack of accountability. The bureaucratic machinery in India was notorious for its cumbersome procedures, excessive regulations, and bureaucratic red tape. Lengthy bureaucratic processes, multiple layers of approvals, and all kinds of hurdles hampered the growth of business, investment, and economic development, leading to inefficiencies and delays.

Add to this the fact that bureaucrats, thanks to a lackadaisical government, enjoyed a considerable degree of autonomy and discretion in their roles, and hence were rarely made accountable. Delays in approvals, project clearances, and implementation of policies hindered governance effectiveness, infrastructure development, and service delivery, impeding the country's progress. Most people believed that government functionaries were not diligent or disciplined. Files would take ages to clear, and governance suffered. A bureaucrat once told me, 'One way to get some under-the-table money is to just not clear the files. Someone will come seeking it and will understand the intentions of the man in charge. Such brazenness stemmed from the lethargy at the very top in the executive.'

Modi's transformation of Gujarat gave hope to the common man—that India too can transform. His speeches and ideas reinforced this belief, and, hence, people were ready to make Modi their man of the moment. His emphasis on the transition towards digitalization, transparency, and citizen-centric governance showed that here was a politician who was laying the groundwork for further reforms in the years to come. People believed that he would address these challenges and propel India towards a more efficient, transparent, and accountable administrative framework. It was an approach by a leader that had not been seen in India before. Laying a blueprint for an efficient and strong India for Indians—this was what a population tired of corruption wanted desperately. This was what a young and restless generation that would be voting for the first time wanted. This vision and clarity of intent were what India needed. And, hence, 2014 would prove to be a landmark year—politically and emotionally.

Party	Seats won
BJP	282
INC	44
Indian National Trinamool Congress	34
Samajwadi Party	5
Bahujan Samajwadi Party	0
All India Anna Dravida Munnetra Kazhagam	37
Bija Janata Dal	20
Telugu Desam Party	16
Shiv Sena	18

Perhaps, for the first time in decades, Indian voters in 2014 cast their ballot with their hearts (for Modi) and with their minds (for economic policy, national security, assertive foreign policy, and corruption-free governance). Additionally, by and large if not altogether, the voting cut across caste lines. If nothing else, this in itself was a spectacular achievement.

3

Crafting a New Sports Ecosystem

I hail from the state that has given the country Neeraj Chopra, the latest poster boy of Indian sports. When he prepares to throw the javelin, his eyes fixed on a point beyond and his hair billowing in the wind, I cross my fingers and hope that he wins a gold medal; competition after competition. Such hope is a long departure from the past, when as Indians, we were happy enough if our athletes could at least touch the qualifying mark (or, just qualify for world-level competitions). Now, we expect them to be on the podium, even in the Olympics. The change in our mindsets is a reflection of a new India that is emerging from the ashes of the past, when just participating in competitions was good enough.

While working on my earlier book *Neeraj Chopra: From Panipat to Podium*, I had the good fortune of listening to the amazing stories of grit and resilience from our sports stars. In fact, those who could not make it to a global stage shared much more intriguing stories of how the system was designed to fail them. And, maybe that's why it became all the more important for me to understand the change that has happened in the last decade.

A friend shared how she grew up listening to the story of 8 August 1984 many times over. She was in her teens then.

The emotion of angst and helplessness that accompanied this story was something I think she could never fathom. But, no matter who asked and when it was retold, the story had the same feel. I could tell, the loss hurt.

Yes, it was the 1984 Olympics and 8 August was when India's ace athlete P.T. Usha missed a bronze in the 400m race, by 1/100th of a second. If anyone, after Milkha Singh, understands the value of a second, it would be P.T. Usha. When I saw the race myself on television years later, I finally understood why as a nation we were so pained by that loss. Because the 1980s was when TV had arrived in most people's homes. Unlike during the Milkha Singh loss in 1960, where India would 'read' about the event, P.T. Usha's loss felt personal. And, if seeing is believing, then seeing victory snatched by a difference of a fraction of a second is truly heartbreaking.

When the dust settled, following many analyses later, we heard that it was not just the restart of the race that had caught her a bit off-guard. The 'Payyoli Express', as she is fondly known, said she could not sustain her energy level in the final stretch of 35 metres due to a diet that she was alien to. In addition, we learnt that if Usha had known about the technicality of close finishes, she would have probably won a bronze! Recall how Romania's Cistieana Cojocaru dipped her chest exactly at the finish line, while P.T. Usha just coasted across, and it was this 1/100th of a second that India shall never forget.

Cut to the 1996 Atlanta Olympics, where Leander Paes won a bronze medal in tennis; the 2000 Sydney Olympics, where Karnam Malleswari won a bronze medal in the women's 69-kg weightlifting category and became the first-ever woman in India to win an Olympic medal; and, then, the 2004 Athens

Olympics, where star shooter Rajyavardhan Singh Rathore (now a BJP leader and minister in Rajasthan; formerly also minister of state (independent charge) for youth and sports affairs) won the silver medal in men's double-trap shooting. These one-off wins by athletes were toasted. But sceptics wondered if that was enough, and whether India, with its sparse wins, should even bother to compete in international events such as the Olympics. Such conversations must have hurt our athletes, who had to not only compete with the best in the world but also tackle all sorts of obstacles back home—the lack of sponsorships, the lack of world-class training facilities, etc.

Then, in the 2008 Beijing Olympics, Vijender Singh got us a bronze in boxing. But the magical moment was when our national anthem, for the first time, reverberated through the stadium, after a very studious-looking Abhinav Bindra won the men's 10-metre air rifle event and became the first Indian to win an individual gold medal at the Olympics. It was a sight to behold, a moment to remember forever. It has been etched in our collective consciousness—his stoic demeanour and the smile!

That said, there was no end to the lingering doubts we had about the fitness, diet, and training that our athletes received. Seen against the backdrop of our rich cricket board, the Board of Control for Cricket in India (BCCI), all other sports paled in comparison. While we continued sending contingents to participate in global championships, our highest number was still below 100. That a country of over a billion people should be sending so few athletes was surely an anomaly. Yet, as athletes kept doing better and other sports, such as badminton, became popular (thanks to the likes of Prakash Padukone and later P. Gopichand, Saina Nehwal, and P.V. Sindhu), the individual perseverance and grit of athletes, with some meagre and token government support, saw Indian sportspersons making a mark on the international stage.

A Paradigm Shift Begins

Things had to change dramatically if the next level was to be breached. That change was waiting in the wings.

In the BJP's manifesto, released before the 2014 elections, a separate section was dedicated to sports. The document outlined how the party's prime ministerial candidate Narendra Modi envisioned the growth of sports in the country. Apart from promising to strengthen India's sports culture and ensure access to sporting facilities for all age groups, the manifesto also spoke of how the BJP, if elected, would promote traditional and modern sports. From ensuring a National Talent Search Programme for sports to setting up academies across the state (while also empowering the states to improve their existing facilities), the sports plan mentioned in the 2014 manifesto was a refreshing change from the past decades of neglect that our sportspersons suffered.

The manifesto also addressed a dire concern of sportspersons, which is, job security. The manifesto promised an attractive career path for sportspersons in the government sector, public sector units, and also the private sector. The BJP, with Modi as its candidate, understood that the youth of the country would take up sports to excel at the highest levels, but that would not be possible if they had to constantly keep looking over their shoulders to make both ends meet.

These promises, as it turned out, were not just on paper. They were delivered in right earnest.

Ever since coming to power in 2014, the Modi government has taken many measures to improve the sports ecosystem of the country. A cursory academic analysis of the government's initiatives in sports tells us that a drastic revolution in sports is underway in India due to these initiatives. Most notably, Khelo India, Target Olympic Podium Scheme, and Fit India Movement have gathered tremendous support from the people of India. These campaigns are dramatically changing the sports landscape of India. From policy interventions to infrastructural advancements and quality training for athletes, the government has focused on improving on all fronts and plugging loopholes that have prevented India from realizing its true potential in international sports.

In 2017, while inaugurating a world-class synthetic track at the P.T. Usha School of Athletics in Kinalur, Kerala, Prime Minister Modi remarked, 'Sports is now a serious career option' for our athletes.[1] The sports ecosystem has indeed undergone a paradigm shift in the past decade under Modi. At the same event, Modi mentioned how India is a sports-loving country.[2] One would wonder why the prime minister should have said so, considering that a billion-people-plus country had just won two medals in the Olympics in the preceding year at Rio de Janeiro. Perhaps, the culture of sports in India from its ancient to medieval period is what prompted him to make that remark. Or, and perhaps also, he wanted to nudge the Indian youngsters and atheletes to achieve glory through sporting successes.

In the Vedic age, the presence of *vyayamshalas* and *akhadas* was a common feature, where people would be trained in yoga, wrestling, and martial arts. Indians, in the ancient era, were experts in games such as chess, chariot race, archery, and mallakhambh, among others.[3] In fact, games such as chess, polo, and snakes and ladders were invented in India before they travelled to other parts of the world and gained popularity.[4]

During the British period, cricket became a widely played game and the post-Independence era saw the emergence of hockey, with the Indian hockey team dominating the event with multiple Olympic gold medals—thanks to the brilliance of players such as Balbir Singh Sr and others. Of course, prior to this was the legendary Dhyan Chand, who mesmerized the hockey world even before India gained Independence. His remarkable exploits at the 1936 Berlin Olympics are still fresh in the hearts and minds of Indian sports enthusiasts. After India's triumph at the 1983 Cricket World Cup held in the UK, cricket too has gone from strength to strength to become the most prominent sport in the country. But let us not forget that in hockey, India remains the most successful team at the Olympics (men's event), having won eight golds, one silver, and one bronze.

At the Tokyo Olympics 2021, India won a historic bronze medal, which was significant because we won a medal after a gap of forty-one years![5] The games also saw India win its first gold in athletics. The star was Neeraj Chopra, and his performance gripped the entire country in a frenzy. Over the years, wrestling has also caught the attention of the people of India with athletes such as Sushil Kumar, Sakshi Malik, Bajrang Punia, and Yogeshwar Dutt winning medals at the Olympics. Kumar remains the most successful amongst the lot, with a silver and bronze medal.

Still, such performances on the international stage were an exception not the norm, as should have been. This would make any well-wisher of Indian sports contemplate: Where did India go wrong? What did India not do right to truly bring the sports potential of India out of the closet?

Decades of Indifference

One can attribute the lack of India's performance over the decades since Independence to the indifference of successive governments in the promotion of sports and apathy towards its athletes. Stories after stories speak about how previous governments mistreated athletes and failed to create a conducive sporting ecosystem in the country.

'He used to get a paltry amount of ₹2200 from the Army, and that too stopped after his death on 3 December 1979. He joined the Army in 1922 during the British Raj. But what did the government do for him in the 32 years he lived in independent India?' says Dhyan Chand's son, Ashok Kumar, also an eminent hockey player, about how his father was treated by the government despite being the country's foremost sports personality.[6]

Similar is the story of India's first individual medallist at the Olympics, K.D. Jadhav, who won a bronze medal in wrestling at the 1952 Helsinki Olympics. Even after that glorious achievement, he received no help and had to sell his wife's jewellery to build a house for himself. Eventually, neglected by successive governments and unrecognized by the very people whom he represented and won a medal for, he died in poverty in his hometown of Karad in 1984.[7]

It was not just governments that were apathetic to the needs of sportspersons. Various sports federations were also unconcerned, busy as they were in promoting their self-interests. The federations had become a den of corruption and nepotism, with power and positions being taken over by a few individuals for long periods. Union Sports Minister Kiren Rijiju even appealed to these federations to take measures in the best interests of the athletes of the country. He said, 'I request and appeal to all the sports federations in India to keep politics away from sports to make sure that the players don't suffer because of them.'[8]

There are several instances of people helming sports federations for long periods with very little accountability. The All India Football Federation, for example, had Congress leader Priya Ranjan Dasmunshi as its president for over two decades. Similar was the case with tennis, where R.K. Khanna served as the president of the All India Tennis Association from 1992 to 2000; and, previously as secretary from 1966 to 1975, and again from 1988 to 1992. The apathy of sports administration in India is incomplete without the mention of Congress leader Suresh Kalmadi, who served as the president of the Indian Olympic Association from 1996 to 2011, which also coincided with his presidency of the Athletics Association of India from 1989 to 2005.[9] Kalmadi was arrested in 2011, in a matter concerning the Commonwealth Games scam.

The dubious nexus of politics and sports administration not only harmed sportspersons and Indian prospects but also turned the federations into dens of corruption and incompetence. Union governments most certainly had a duty to curb this menace and ensure transparency in the functioning of these federations. However, as we saw from the examples mentioned above, members of the government or the party in power were themselves at the helm of affairs at these federations. This made bringing positive changes to their functioning virtually impossible. Further, matters were made worse by the system itself, which placed the least priority on an athlete's well-being.

There was another problem as well: the absence of a credible search programme, both at the national and the state levels, to spot bright talents and bring them to the fore with all the support required. The biggest losers were youngsters from poor and underprivileged families, who had the potential but not the means to showcase their prowess. They had the dreams, the desire, and the ability to put in the hard work needed, but they missed out, simply because there was no proper system in place that was seeking them out.

Athletes who wish to arrive on the national and international stage must begin their training early on in their lives, preferably at the school level itself. There should, thus, have been a convergence of academics and sports. But this was not to be. Indeed, for decades, the mindset was that sports was a pastime, and students must shun it as it came in the way of academics. If this was the case at the school level, things were no better in colleges and universities.

India lacked a national-level sports university that would cater to the needs of budding sportspersons and aspiring coaches. It was only in 2018 that the Government of India announced the setting up of a National Sports University in Imphal, Manipur.[10]

The lack of fruitful interaction between education and sports departments in states and at the Centre kept hurting the aspirations of young athletes, who would eventually give up their ambitions due to the burden of academics or for want of finance. An athlete's well-being was also immensely affected due to the lack of coordination between the state and central authorities, whether at the federation level or the government level. Matters regarding the selection of deserving athletes for competition and providing quality training facilities to the right athletes also suffered due to this lack of communication. Such institutional apathy towards the athletes made families discourage kids from pursuing sports as a career and focus on academics instead.

And, it is here that the (flawed) saying, '*Padhoge likhoge banoge nawab, kheloge kudoge banoge kharab*' (You will succeed if you study, and be a failure if you take to sports) became sort of institutionalized in the minds of the people. Such dismissal of sports as a career option resulted in India lacking a sports culture, where budding athletes could be trained from childhood and be given all requisite opportunities to excel at the international level.

Parents too were not really bothered if the schools they admitted their wards into had sports grounds or sports coaches. With little pressure on them, most schools did not care to equip their facilities with playfields or hire trainers. This would further result in a lack of physical education teachers in schools; and, wherever they existed, the quality was far from being acceptable. This situation did not improve at the university level either. In global sporting nations, such as the US, China, or Australia, many university-goers are also international athletes, who train at the inbuilt university facilities. However, India did not have a single such university that could claim to have world-class sports training facilities.

Even if quality athletes made it to university and remained dedicated to their sport, they were rarely encouraged to take the game a notch higher and aim for Olympic or world-championship-level participation. This mediocrity syndrome was like the final nail in the coffin of aspirations for young Indian athletes. The academic schedule of the university also made many school-level athletes invariably give up sports at the university level—a phase that mattered the most in a professional sports career.

The near absence of institutional support for athletes in India meant that they could not receive quality coaching either. There was always a severe shortage of quality coaches, right from the junior to the national level. The predominant reason for this was twofold. First, the salary of coaches in India was insignificant to the extent that a professional coach would find it difficult to sustain a family of four if they adopted coaching as a full-time career. Second, there were very few options for aspiring coaches to be trained at quality facilities. Except for Netaji Subhas National Institute of Sports (NIS), Patiala, India did not have a single other centre where coaches could be trained professionally and given opportunities to grow to an international level. This was a tremendous impediment for not just aspiring coaches but also for athletes who would have liked to train under Indian coaches.

This sorry state of affairs meant that those Indian athletes, who would make it to the international level, would have to invariably hire a foreign coach to stay on top of their game. The foreign coaches came with their own challenges, the most significant one being language. The language barrier became a problem for both the athlete and the coach alike. Moreover, Indian athletes were used to a certain sports culture in India, which was alien to what the foreign coaches brought; they expected the Indians to come to terms with the Western methods of training. Hence, such arrangements also were difficult to stitch for a longer period. The government also fell behind in supporting former players to set up academies and train young athletes.

It is only in the recent past that the Modi-led government has supported former athletes like P.T. Usha, Anju Bobby George, and Gagan Narang to set up academies and reach out to young athletes. The government sanctioned funds for not just the establishment of such academies but also the upgradation of existing facilities and smooth functioning of the academy. Such initiatives augur well for budding athletes who would want to train under legends of Indian sports and also get access to world-class training facilities. Here, one must also mention the excellent work that badminton ace P. Gopichand has done with his academy, which has produced world-class players, both in the men's and women's categories.

While interacting with India's Asian Games contingent in 2014, Prime Minister Modi said to the medal winners, 'It creates self-pride in the hearts of all Indians, your efforts produce honour.'[11] His remark left the athletes 'very motivated' by the 'fantastic experience' of meeting the country's prime minister.[12]

New Initiatives

Such interactions were followed by the implementation of some praiseworthy initiatives mentioned earlier. The Target Olympic Podium Scheme (TOPS), which was launched in July 2014, is aimed at helping Indian athletes secure, as the name suggests, an Olympic podium finish. This flagship scheme of the Ministry of Youth Affairs and Sports is divided into two groups—Core and Development. The core group contains elite athletes, such as Neeraj Chopra, P.V. Sindhu, and Meerabai Chanu, among others, while the Development group covers young and upcoming athletes, such as Rohit Yadav and Jeswin Aldrin, among others.

Within two years of its launch, at the Rio Olympics, the only two medallists that India saw—P.V. Sindhu in badminton and Sakshi Mallik in wrestling—were both TOPS athletes. Post Rio, the Ministry of Youth Affairs and Sports made several administrative and policy changes to the scheme, among which was the inclusion of a dedicated TOPS secretariat under the Sports Authority of India (SAI) with its

CEO at the helm. Such changes meant that India gave its best Olympics performance in the next Olympics at Tokyo 2020 (held in July–August 2021), with seven medals and a historic gold in the javelin throw.

Not just the seven medal winners, but the entire Indian contingent was covered under TOPS before the Tokyo Olympics, which highlighted the government's intent of giving the best facilities for the chosen athletes. The benefits of TOPS have also been extended to para-athletes. In the Tokyo Paralympics 2020, the entire Indian contingent of fifty-four para-athletes was covered by TOPS, and it turned out to be the country's best performance ever at the Paralympics. India finished with nineteen medals, up from the four that were won in the Rio Olympics in 2016.

The success of TOPS ever since the overhaul of the scheme after Rio is also attributed to the establishment of the Mission Olympic Cell (MOC) of TOPS, which is under the chairmanship of the director-general of SAI. MOC discusses athletes' progress, training requirements, and plans with not just the athletes but also their coaches. This interaction helps in planning the support to be given to TOPS athletes more efficiently, as the coaches have hands-on knowledge of an athlete's preparedness for competitions.

The MOC has also been instrumental in enhancing the channels of communication between athletes and the government, should they wish to place any request regarding their training or finances before the relevant ministry. It is the MOC that hears these requests and approves them for further action, whenever it deems fit, in the best interest of the athlete. The system of dialogue has resulted in a greater dialogue between the stakeholders and the elimination of, or at least a reduction in, misunderstandings.

One of the outcomes of such discussions was that in September 2017, the Ministry of Youth Affairs and Sports announced that the core group of TOPS athletes would receive ₹50,000 every month for out-of-pocket expenses and the Development group athletes would be given ₹25,000 every month to ease any financial strain that they might be facing.[13]

With the support system for elite athletes taken care of by TOPS, the next important aspect that the government focused on was to reach the masses with sports facilities and create world-class tournaments wherein athletes from across the country could participate. This was done through the Khelo India scheme, which came into being after combining three existing schemes—Rajiv Gandhi Khel Abhiyan, Urban Sports Infrastructure Scheme, and National Sports Talent Search Scheme. These three schemes had failed to deliver on their expected outcomes, and, hence, a total revamp was essential.

The government, through Khelo India, hopes to revive the sports culture in the country by encouraging more and more youngsters to take up sports—and take it up as a serious career option. The first Khelo India tournament was the Khelo India School Games, held in 2018. In 2019, it was renamed as Khelo India Youth Games; it saw the participation of 5,925 athletes in 2020. The government also announced the Khelo India University Games for university students, with the first edition taking place in 2021 in Odisha. Subsequent editions were hosted in Bengaluru and Lucknow. The quality of the competition and the facilities provided to athletes have kept getting better every year and have now begun to yield results.

In the World University Games held in 2023 in China, India finished seventh, winning twenty-six medals. What makes this performance special is the fact that since the inception of these Games in 1959, India won eighteen medals across all editions. However, just in this one edition, India won more medals than all previous performances combined; surely, this was an indicator of changing times for Indian sports.[14] The efforts of the union government are praiseworthy, particularly concerning the Khelo India scheme, as it has successfully got the states on board to enhance sporting facilities at the grassroots.

Through Khelo India, state-level centres have been upgraded for high-performance training in addition to the upgradation of SAI Extension Centres to Khelo India Centres. The reason for such upgradation is to maintain a certain standard of facilities at these centres that athletes can avail of daily. Athletes who train at SAI Extension Centres are given a sports kit worth ₹5,000, a stipend of ₹10,000 per trainee for ten months a year, and infrastructural support of ₹5,000 per trainee, thereby providing institutional support for their sporting ambitions.[15]

The Khelo India scheme also initiated a dedicated talent search and development programme. Across twenty selected disciplines, the selected athletes are given financial assistance of ₹500,000 per annum for eight years. The choice of eight years per athlete is done to ensure a long-term commitment to the athletes in terms of their training requirements and competition exposure. The aim now is to catch budding athletes at a tender age, give them the appropriate training, and prepare them for the international stage. Examples of young archers such as Ojas Deotale and Aditi Swami, who won gold in the men's and women's individual compound events at world championships, respectively, are testament to the success of the Khelo India scheme.

Another very important aspect of Khelo India is the promotion of traditional sports. Sports that originated in India, such as Mallakhambh, Yogasana, Silambam, Kalaripayattu, Gatka, and Thang Ta, are being promoted throughout the country, and regular competitions to increase awareness about these sports have also been conducted. To ensure the success of its sports initiatives, the government realized that a culture of fitness also needs to be inculcated among the people of India. Hence, the prime minister launched the Fit India Movement in August 2019. The idea was to make fitness an integral part of the daily lives of the people of India. A large number of celebrities endorsed his message, posting videos of their activities to promote fitness. It was not long before it became a people's movement.

To achieve the objectives of the Fit India Movement, the government has been organizing various events across the country to bring together people and make fitness fun and easy. Fit India Freedom Run, Fit India Plog Run, Fit India Mobile App to help users with diet plans and exercises, Fit India Quiz, Fit India School Week, Fit India School Certification, and the appointment of Fit India ambassadors are some of the programmes executed to help people of the country realize the importance of fitness.

The Fit India Movement, much like the Swachh Bharat Abhiyaan, aims to bring a behavioural change in the people of India. Issues of fitness have never been addressed since Independence, and, hence, they didn't find any mention as a priority with earlier governments. To initiate a programme and keep it running to achieve a behavioural change is a significant move by the Modi government for the overall welfare of India.

Policy analysts would be baffled by the remarkable change in the sports apparatus of the country in less than a decade. What made the recent transformation possible is the political will of the government to change things for the better, especially the involvement of the prime minister. Modi has been personally involved in supervising the welfare of the athletes and has stepped in whenever any athlete has requested help. His vision for sports has been complemented by the administrative acumen of the sports ministers chosen by him, who have implemented the schemes with an efficiency that had been missing in previous governments.

The interactions of the prime minister with athletes before and after any international event, such as the Olympics, Commonwealth Games, and Asian Games, have left an indelible mark in their hearts and minds. When the prime minister met the men's hockey team after their record bronze medal performance at Tokyo, goalkeeper P.R. Sreejesh said, 'He didn't make us feel like we were talking to the Prime Minister. He spoke very openly, in a very friendly manner, and he took us in[to] our comfort zone.'[16]

Para-athletes too have had the opportunity for such interactions with the prime minister. Indian para table tennis star, Bhavina Patel, mentioned how 'talking with Prime Minister Modi gives us the motivation to do better'.[17] It's a clear indication of the prime minister's personal connection with the athletes. Para legend Devendra Jhajharia has often mentioned how the prime minister not only listened to his suggestions on para facilities in India but also implemented them for the ease of para-athletes. He also shared how his family was part of interactions with the prime minister and how glad he felt to have had an opportunity to speak with the highest political office holder of the country.[18]

The rise of sports culture in India has transcended geographical boundaries, with smaller towns and rural areas also witnessing a surge in sporting activities. Grassroots-level initiatives, coupled with the accessibility of digital platforms for training and coaching, have democratized sports participation, allowing talent from every corner of the country to shine. India's journey towards enhancing its sports culture is marked by significant progress and promise. With concerted efforts from the government, sports bodies, educational institutions, and the private sector, India is poised to emerge as a sporting powerhouse on the global stage. As the nation continues to celebrate its sporting heroes and invest in the development of infrastructure and talent, the future of Indian sports looks brighter than ever before.

Khelo India has played a significant role in promoting sports culture in India. It has raised awareness about the importance of sports and fitness among the youth and has encouraged a shift from traditional academic-centric pursuits to sports. The programme has also created employment opportunities in the sports sector. With the development of sports infrastructure and the increasing emphasis on sports coaching and training, there is a growing demand for coaches, trainers, and other sports-related professionals. It has been instrumental in revitalizing the sports ecosystem in India and has laid the foundation for the country to emerge as a major force in the international sporting arena.[19]

It can be said that the political will, personal touch, and administrative acumen of the prime minister have been of tremendous importance in the ongoing changes in the sports ecosystem of the country. The revolution, which has been set rolling since 2014, is a result of the extraordinary vision of the government and its ability to gather all stakeholders together to bring about a positive change in the way India sees and pursues sports.

India is on its way to becoming a globally recognized sports power, and it is only a matter of time before India will stake its rightful claim as a sports power. When that happens, Indians will be sure to look back at the policy interventions and their implementation by the Modi government, which enabled the country to emerge as a sporting power. Until then, the government and all stakeholders must remain dedicated to continue with sincere efforts to keep improving every day and ensuring the overall well-being of all athletes of the country.

4

Leave No One Behind

'The tea is fantastic, thank you.'[1]

The nation watched a calm, stoic, unafraid Wing Commander Abhinandan Varthaman make the polite remark while in Pakistan's custody for a little over sixty hours. Wing Commander Abhinandan's MiG-21 Bison had been shot down after it had successfully intercepted a posse of Pakistani fighters over the Line of Control in the Rajouri-Mendhar sector on 17 February 2019, a day after the Balakot strike. Before the Indian Air Force (IAF) pilot was ejected from his MiG-21, he shot down a fourth-generation F-16 fighter. He was captured by villagers in Pakistan-occupied Kashmir, where he landed, and was handed over to the Pakistani military.

The story goes that after Prime Minister Modi saw images of the bleeding Indian pilot and his smiling captors gloating over their success, he told the Indian intelligence top brass to unequivocally inform Pakistan that New Delhi would stop at nothing if Abhinandan was harmed and not released immediately.

(Interestingly, in a different context and on a different occasion, Modi had a message for Pakistan, which often reminded India of being a nuclear-weapon state: 'Our nuclear weapon arsenal is not for Diwali.')[2]

This stern message was promptly conveyed by the then chief of Research and Analysis Wing (RAW), India's external intelligence service, Anil Dhasmana, to his then counterpart in Pakistan's Inter-Services Intelligence (ISI), Lt General Syed Asim Munir Ahmed Shah, over a secure line.

Dhasmana was so blunt that even the ISI chief was surprised by the firm tone of the RAW chief. As if to dispel any doubts that may have still existed in Pakistan's mind, the RAW head warned him that Islamabad would face consequences if the Indian officer was not handed over unharmed, and without delay. At other times, Pakistan would have perhaps taken the threat with a pinch of salt. But with Modi at the helm … well, things were different.

To demonstrate that India meant business, the country's armed forces were ordered to prepare the mobile Prithvi ballistic missile batteries in the Rajasthan sector. It set alarm bells ringing in faraway Washington as well.[3]

Soon enough, Pakistan's prime minister at the time, Imran Khan, directed that the Indian officer be released. He made the announcement in the National Assembly on 28 February, calling the decision 'a gesture of peace'.[4] It was a face-saving remark. In reality, as subsequent accounts that came into the public domain showed, Pakistan had been rattled.

What followed was a dramatic sequence of events that not only gripped the attention of the world but also showcased India's power of assertive diplomacy and the resilience of the human spirit. It was a release if not an evacuation that showed how every single Indian life mattered.

As it happened, I had an opportunity to interact with many officers of the Indian Foreign Service in 2022–2023. The group, though mostly comprising senior officers and recent retirees, also had some younger-generation officers who were still learning the tricks of a skilled Indian diplomat on the field. The topic of the conversation was wide-ranging—from changing foreign policy to diaspora interactions, the status of India in the modern world, and the impact of Prime Minister Modi on contemporary geopolitics.

However, what struck me as being most remarkable was the changed perception in the group. Everybody said that here was a government that would reach out and help every single Indian in distress in any part of the world. This was when India was still reeling or steadily stepping out of the COVID-19 challenges. And, to achieve that objective, everything, from gentle diplomacy to coercion, would be applied. Indians in trouble would be evacuated from the remotest corners of the world and brought back safe and sound.

It was in this context that the Abhinandan incident came to mind. This was a case of an officer of the Indian Air Force. Ordinary Indians too have been evacuated in times of crisis, with the same care and concern. Indians caught in war zones, Indians stuck due to a pandemic—the cause could be any, but the action from the Indian government was unfailing. That brings us to the question: Was such a brave and humanitarian approach also evident during previous governments?

The Rule of Apathy

While the issue of the large Indian diaspora has been discussed in a later chapter, it is important here to understand that for long, Indians across the world, including those who had moved abroad for economic opportunities a few generations ago, were not considered a priority by the Indian government. It's not that there was some policy to that effect. But actions spoke louder than words. For instance, in the early 1950s, when anti-Indian sentiments started brewing among indigenous Africans, it provoked attacks on Indians who had flourishing businesses in countries such as Mozambique, Kenya, Zambia, and Uganda. Yet, the government of the day 'pledged solidarity with the African cause', even if it meant abandoning the interest of Indian settlers in East Africa. In later years, Prime Minister Nehru, apparently getting somewhat impatient with Indians in the African continent, even went to the extent of declaring in Parliament that 'they [Indians] could expect no help from us, no protection from us if they seek any special rights in Africa, which were not in the interests of Africa'.[5]

In August 1972, after General Idi Amin, the commander of the Ugandan army, staged a coup d'état, assuming control of the country, he declared a 'war for the economic liberation' from Indians. All non-citizens were notified to leave the country within ninety days, fanning the flames of widespread 'Indophobia'. Consequently, nearly 55,000 persons of Indian origin (PIOs) and 5,000 Indian nationals were deported and their properties confiscated. 'India however could not offer either cash or accommodation facilities; we simply advised them to re-join their families in India.'[6] Only about 5,000 of the deported Indians came to temporarily stay in India. Clearly, more could have been done for them.

This was standard reaction of the government in those days to people of Indian origin. Our governments did not give non-resident Indians (NRIs) and persons of Indian origin (PIOs) the priority they deserved. Perhaps, there were larger issues that former leaders considered important. However, when in distress, if your country of origin does not help you, it is indeed a sad situation. On the other hand, Hollywood films depicted how the US used all its might to save and extract its citizens. We watched in awe and hoped that someday India too would stand up for her citizens in distress.

Before 2014, there had been some attempts at evacuations, and successful ones too. However, a lot of these efforts were limited and lacked a coherent vision from the government. Government officials who had India's best interests at heart prompted the politicians of the day to take action. In other words, the Indian government had to be prodded and cajoled to do something on its own. For instance, the government evacuated Indians from Iraq in 1980 and Yemen in 1986. However, the most well-known and documented evacuation process was the Kuwait airlift, popularly known as the 'Gulf Airlift' of 1990. As the then dictator Saddam Hussein's forces moved towards Kuwait in August of that year, a human tragedy of disastrous dimensions began unfolding—one that hadn't been witnessed since the Great Ethiopian Famine. Trapped in no-man's land on the border between Iraq and Jordan, over 80,000 refugees became helpless pawns in this crisis. A majority of those refugees happened to be Indians.

Pregnant women were fainting because of the high temperatures, and hundreds of babies had no milk to drink. The matter became more serious with limited sanitation facilities and few medical personnel to offer support. Food was scarce, and even water had to be paid for. It was what came to be called 'hell on earth'.[7] In the face of this monumental humanitarian crisis, the Government of India's response was baffling. The then External Affairs Minister, I.K. Gujral, brought back only 300 odd Indians from war-torn Kuwait, and nearly all were VIPs! This return flight came to be infamously called 'the millionaire's flight'.[8]

A businessman, who had lived in Kuwait for two decades before the crisis, remembered, 'When we asked him what would happen to our investments in Kuwait, Gujral replied, "I told you for so many years to invest in India. You did not listen to me. Now you will have to suffer."'

Eventually, the government embarked on the biggest air evacuation exercise to extricate the Indians who were stuck there. While military aircraft were considered to airlift them out of the country, Air India made the evacuations possible. Buses full of Indians were driven to Jordan for the flights back home, which took off from its capital Amman. In around sixty days, Air India (along with Indian Airlines) operated 488 flights that brought stranded Indians back home. The so-called success would be lauded for years. But, as a recent Hindi film showed, the evacuation exercise became possible due to a partnership of private and public individuals; the government was quick to, however, take the credit!

Decades later, the government faced criticism at home for failing to evacuate citizens swiftly out of Libya when that country was on the brink of a civil war in 2011. By contrast, other countries had had been prompt in moving their citizens out. 'Out of Libya India crawls, the rest are safe at home', the *Indian Express* commented, adding that India remained the only major country with thousands of nationals stranded there.[9] According to a report in Reuters, 'China, meanwhile, evacuated 32,000 of its citizens in an operation involving four heavy-lift IL-76 military aircraft, chartered aircraft, and a navy frigate.'[10] After much foot-dragging, the Indian government launched Operation Safe Homecoming and chartered Air India and other commercial flights along with passenger ships to move out the stranded Indian citizens.

There have been a few other attempts, like in 1994, when India evacuated 1,700 of the 7,000 NRIs in Yemen on IAF and Air India flights. Similarly, in 1996, more than 45,000 emergency certificates were issued to Indians wishing to leave the UAE before the expiration of an amnesty period for illegal foreigners. In July 2006, due to a conflict between Israel and Lebanon, thousands of Indians were stuck in these foreign lands. Upon hearing of this, the government organized Operation Sukoon from Lebanon. The Indian Navy took up the task.

Three Indian warships and a fleet tanker—the destroyer *INS Mumbai*, two frigates, *INS Brahmaputra* and *INS Betwa*, and the fleet tanker *INS Shakti*—were returning from a goodwill trip to Greece. Consequently, about 2,300 Indians were evacuated. The Ministry of External Affairs also lent support for evacuations from Kyrgyzstan in June 2010 and from Egypt in January–February 2011.

In the Modi Era

However, it was only during the prime ministership of Modi that the response to evacuations saw a significant shift, demonstrating a proactive approach to addressing challenges, leveraging diplomatic channels, deploying resources, and coordinating with international partners to execute large-scale evacuation operations with efficiency and precision. There have been so many evacuation operations over the last decade that it has become difficult to tell each story.

Each had different challenges attached to them. From facing natural disasters to political unrest, Indians stranded in foreign lands have found reassurance in the swift and decisive actions taken by the Modi government to bring them home. While every such instance has seen intense negotiations and convoluted scenarios, there are still some parallels that can be drawn—the most important of them being the Indian government's operating principle: No Indian should be left behind. One of the biggest transitions in India's engagement with her diaspora is the shift from a passive to a proactive and humanitarian approach. It was soon after the Modi government came to power that this skill was evident.

From the Clutches of the Taliban

Jesuit priest Father Alexis Prem Kumar was abducted by the Taliban in 2014. On 2 June, the forty-seven-year-old Afghanistan director of the Jesuit Refugee Service (JRS) was kidnapped by unidentified gunmen in the Herat province of western Afghanistan. Although Afghanistan was being ruled by a democratically elected president, the Taliban had a noticeable presence in the province, and it was said that Prem Kumar had been abducted by that organization.

Prem Kumar was on a visit to a school in Sohadat, some 25 km from Herat, which was managed by JRS, an international Catholic organization looking out for the interests of the refugees and the forcibly displaced. The school was meant for children of refugee families returning from Iran and for those in the neighbouring villages. According to sources, Prem Kumar had been informed about the threats to his life, particularly in light of the attack on the Indian consulate on 23 May, which was successfully defended. However, he stepped out of the safe limits of Herat and was taken hostage.

Under Prime Minister Modi's leadership and then External Affairs Minister Sushma Swaraj's deft diplomacy, the long process of locating, negotiating, and bringing back Prem Kumar began. The ministry got in touch with

Afghan authorities and Americans and began taking regular updates from the Afghan police. With pressure from the Indian government mounting, the Afghan authorities arrested a person who had helped the six gunmen abduct Prem Kumar.

More accomplices were nabbed to find out about the possible hideouts or safe houses for the Taliban militants. Ajit Doval, who was appointed as India's 5th National Security Advisor on 30 May 2014, began a special operation. Different ministries, intelligence agencies, and networks of agents and information hunters worked with a singular focus: find and bring Prem Kumar back, safe. Persistence was the key, which ultimately led intelligence and security agencies in the region to locate him and thereafter negotiate his release. After eight months in captivity, the Taliban released Prem Kumar in Helmand, Afghanistan. He said, 'I want to thank the Almighty. Also, this is because of our Prime Minister Modi that I am here.'[11]

Father Alexis Prem Kumar expressed his gratitude towards the prime minister in an interaction with the media after his release in February 2015. After eight months of captivity, he was finally free. Modi called the priest's family on a Sunday afternoon, and when Prem Kumar's father Anthony picked up the phone, the prime minister himself was on the line. Prem Kumar's brother John Joseph had this to say: 'My father cannot speak English. So, my sister Elizabeth took the call. Mr Modi said, "Your brother is alive, safe, and is returning to India. Are you happy?" My sister said, "Yes."'[12]

Finally, in Delhi, Prem Kumar was reunited with his family. Smiling broadly—his face showing palpable relief—he insisted that he was back because of Prime Minister Modi.

Rescued from ISIS Clutches

This was not the only heroic rescue. The prime minister's unconventional methods of diplomacy and engagement were put to the test by a jihadist militant group in West Asia located thousands of kilometres from the Indian subcontinent—the Islamic State in Iraq and the Levant (ISIL), variously called Islamic State in Iraq and Syria (ISIS), Islamic State (IS), or by its Arabic name, Daesh.

ISIS went on a rampage in June 2014, when it launched the Northern Iraq offensive to drive out Iraqi security forces from key areas and capture major Iraqi cities, including Mosul. Then, on 11 June, ISIS took control of Tikrit. Caught in this conflict between the Iraqi forces and ISIS were forty-six Indian nurses—except for one, all of them were from Kerala. Thirty-three of them arrived in August 2013, while thirteen nurses had come in early February 2014. They had been recruited by a Delhi-based agency that charged around ₹1.5 lakh per nurse and promised a salary of $750 (₹45,000 in 2014).

This was a far cry from the meagre monthly salary of less than ₹6,000 that they earned in their home state, which had forced them to seek work in the Gulf nations and earn better remunerations to repay debts and loans. In fact, this is a well-accepted and established process even today.

The nurses were reportedly interviewed by the health ministry of Iraq before they were assigned to a posting at Tikrit Teaching Hospital. After joining the hospital, the building and its immediate premises became their home. Security concerns restrained them from venturing out. As one of them recalled, 'We were never allowed to go out.

Our familiarity with the town was only the skyline we could see from the windows on the second floor, where all the nurses stayed—six in each room.'[13]

On the night of 12 June 2014, hospital staff, including Indian and Iraqi nurses, heard bullets being fired near the hospital. Soon, a building set on fire lit up the night sky. For many nurses, the sight was their first encounter with the growing lawlessness in Iraq and the country's evolving political reality. A hushed discussion among the staff was followed by the Iraqi nurses immediately fleeing the hospital. The Indians, however, had nowhere to go. Far from home, they were stranded in a strange city.

The next day, ISIS militants occupied the ground floor of the hospital. As the gunfight became intense, hospital staff, including the doctors, shifted to the second floor. Marina Jose, a senior nurse from the group, recalled, 'Masked militants with guns often came upstairs to ask us to check on the patients downstairs. Terrified, we would accompany them and do as we were told. Within ten days, everyone had cleared out of the hospital, except us, the Indian nurses.'[14]

Thanks to the internet, the terrified nurses reached out and contacted the Indian authorities. On 13 June, they called Ajay Kumar, the then Indian ambassador in Baghdad, and also reached out to Oommen Chandy, who was then the chief minister of Kerala. Their call for help was quickly relayed to the Government of India. Meanwhile, the International Committee of the Red Cross (ICRC) brought food, basic necessities, and phone recharge vouchers for the staff. These vouchers, data plans, and the power to charge phones ensured that the nurses kept the Indian government apprised of the developments.

The government opened formal and informal channels of communication with countries in the region, including Iraq. With clear directions from Prime Minister Modi that the nurses had to be rescued at all costs. The government also opened backchannel contacts with ISIS and other splinter groups in Iraq. Notably, the intense negotiations that ensued with various interlocutors helped India's case. The government also reached out to its partners in the region. Key businessmen, particularly prominent Malayalis, assisted with providing useful contacts in the region. All these efforts converged into a well-networked system of information sharing, which aided the evacuation strategy.

The conflict, however, worsened before the nurses could get some respite. Despite having lost control of the city and hospital, Iraqi security forces fought pitched battles with ISIS. On 2 July, the hospital building was bombed, severely damaging the emergency ward and the blood bank. The relentless firing and bombing in the area made the building shake and tremble.

On 3 July, some militants asked the nurses to get ready fast as they would be shifted to Mosul, about 200 km from Tikrit. The nurses reached out to the Indian authorities, who asked them to request if their captors could shift them to Erbil instead, as Mosul had fallen and was under ISIS control. The ISIS men conceded to the nurses' demand. The militants fired some shots at the window and the wall behind the nurses to threaten and rush them. With some nurses injured and all of them thoroughly terrified, they hurried onto a bus, which left the hospital at 11.30 in the morning.

Only about thirty minutes into the journey, the nurses learnt that they were actually headed for Mosul, not Erbil. This new information was quickly and secretly relayed to the

Indian ambassador in Iraq by the women sitting in the last rows. The bus reached Mosul at 7.45 p.m. But that was not the only development on 3 July. That fateful Thursday night, the Indian government reached a major breakthrough—a top-secret deal to release the nurses was struck with the ISIS captors through a set of intermediaries. Sushma Swaraj was up until 2.00 a.m. the following day, receiving updates on developments while the deal was being negotiated and finalized by the officials concerned.

The following day, ISIS brought the nurses to the Mosul border and handed them over to the Indian rescue team waiting there. India's intelligence officials, who acted on all information with apt interventions in Iraq, then took the nurses to Erbil airport, from where they awaited their return flight to India.

Interestingly, when the special flight reached Erbil to bring back the nurses, one of them fainted with disbelief! For these nurses, life had been so tricky, scary, and challenging in the last few weeks that they could scarcely believe that they had been rescued. She was revived and escorted into the aircraft by the other nurses in the group. While the aircraft was being refuelled, one of the nurses shared that about fifty more Indians were waiting outside the airport gate. Most of them were from Kerala, much like the officer who had gone to rescue them. The Malayali connection worked. He got them on board as well. The team walked into the aircraft, locked it, and everyone flew back to safety, to India.

It was only a few days later that the herculean diplomatic effort behind the scenes came to light, and the story unfolded. Notably, by the end of June 2014, the situation in Iraq looked bleak. The prime minister then asked Doval to convene a high-level meeting to discuss the latest intelligence on Tikrit and Mosul, besides preparing for the mass evacuation of Indians in Iraq. Reportedly, a day after the meeting, with clear directions from the prime minister, Doval went on a top-secret mission to Iraq.

On arrival, Doval analyzed the situation on the ground and made high-level contacts with the Iraqis. He later reached Damascus and used key Syrian intelligence assets to contact ISIS. According to reports, Indian authorities worked 'closely with the Kurdish authorities to allow the nurses to enter Erbil, and then convinced them to let a special Air India flight to land there.'[15] The identities of the interlocutors, however, were kept secret to enable their engagement in future assignments. Interestingly, there were at least twenty-five meetings in two weeks in response to the crisis.

What I have observed since Modi became the prime minister is that he takes a personal interest in ensuring that whenever an Indian is in distress and needs the government's support, the leadership takes charge and ensures safe passage. Furthermore, such evacuation efforts have left a legacy of preparedness and resilience. Lessons learnt from past evacuations have led to the refinement of protocols and procedures, ensuring that India is better equipped to handle similar situations in the future. The commitment to the safety and well-being of Indian citizens abroad remains a cornerstone of Prime Minister Modi's administration.

One of the most notable instances of India's commitment to ensuring the safety of its citizens abroad was witnessed during the COVID-19 pandemic. As countries around the world imposed lockdowns and travel restrictions, thousands of Indians found themselves stranded in various parts of the globe. In response, the Indian government launched the Vande Bharat Mission, one of the largest repatriation exercises in history, to bring back Indians from different countries. Let us see how those operations unfolded over the decade because it is this experience of operations that makes the more recent ones stand out.

Operation Raahat

Starting in December 2010, the Arab Spring broke out. It was a series of pro-democracy uprisings that enveloped several largely Muslim countries, including Tunisia, Morocco, Bahrain, Egypt, Libya, and Syria, toppling some long-standing authoritarian regimes. Yemen, situated on the southern end of the Arabian Peninsula, witnessed similar demonstrations when young, urban Yemenis took to the streets, demanding the ouster of President Ali Abdullah Saleh. By 2012, Saleh was forced to step down and was succeeded by the Saudi-backed Abdrabbuh Mansur Hadi.

Three years later, rebels called Houthis—an Islamist political-military movement led by the Zaidi Shia Houthis tribe that emerged in North Yemen in the 1990s—pushed out President Hadi, and the country began imploding. Hadi found himself in the middle of the Yemeni civil war, wherein the Houthis began exerting control over large parts of the country.

Anticipating violence, the Indian Ministry of External Affairs issued an advisory to Indian expats in January 2015: they should avoid travelling to Yemen. Further, Indian nationals were asked to avoid conflict areas and remain in contact with the Embassy of India (EOI) in the Yemeni capital of Sanaa. The EOI also set up helplines to assist Indians. Less than two months later, another advisory was issued, which was followed by an urgent advisory on 25 March, urging all Indian citizens to evacuate as soon as possible. The situation in Yemen had gotten worse and violent. Factional wars were erupting in the streets and Indians there had nowhere to turn to.

Operation Raahat was launched in mission mode for evacuations from Yemen. 'It was such an operation that the US and the UK told us that they were not being able to evacuate their nationals. Only India could do it,' said then External Affairs Minister Sushma Swaraj, on Operation Raahat.[16] On 26 March, Saudi Arabia, in response to requests from President Hadi, led a coalition of nine countries (from North Africa and West Asia) in a military intervention, code-named Operation Decisive Storm. This intervention involved bombing locations strategically important to the Houthis. The large military action left millions, including 5,000 Indians, in the midst of a humanitarian crisis.

EAM Sushma Swaraj and General V.K. Singh, then the minister of state for external affairs, swung into action. Officers of the ministry and defence forces, including Chief of Naval Staff Admiral R.K. Dhowan and Chief of Air Staff Air Chief Marshal Arup Raha, played significant roles in the rescue mission. A plan was quickly prepared to evacuate the stranded Indians through Muscat in Oman, which shares a 300-km border with Yemen in the west. For this, two Air India aircraft were flown into Muscat. However, the situation arising out of a desert storm, including a no-fly zone over Yemen, rendered the plan untenable. Even more, two flights with this long a duration were not enough.

It was then that the possibility of flights taking off from Djibouti started being considered. A micro-state with less than a million people and modest facilities at the airport, port, and hotels, Djibouti is situated in the Horn of Africa, with Somalia to its south and Eritrea to its north. It has the Red Sea and the Gulf of Aden to its east, making it strategically important. African nations (like Eritrea and Somalia) share maritime borders with Yemen, thus making it relatively safe and also the nearest country across the Gulf of Aden.

Sanjay Verma—the then Indian ambassador to Ethiopia with concurrent accreditation to Djibouti—informed the ministry that the Indian Navy could also use the Djibouti port as their base. Subsequently, Verma shifted base to Djibouti on 30 March. A control room was established at Hotel Djibouti Palace Kempinski in Djibouti. Since Yemen could not be approached through a land route, it was decided to launch a joint air and sea evacuation from Djibouti. Thereafter, the Indian Navy started the evacuation campaign with the guided missile destroyer *INS Mumbai* and the state-of-the-art frigate *INS Tarkash*, along with two luxurious passenger ships, *MV Kavaratti* and *MV Corals*.

General V.K. Singh was sent to Djibouti to oversee and supervise the entire operation. Being conscious of the limited facilities, the team available there, led by him, booked two hotels. With other logistical arrangements in place, Operation Raahat was launched. It involved the deployment of warships of the Indian Navy. This had to coincide with the evacuees near the Yemeni coast reaching the ports (Aden, Mukalla, and Al-Hudaydah). It was a logistical nightmare, given the failing communication links with Yemen, the dearth of reliable sources of information, and the near absence of community coordinators to mobilize the movements to Yemeni ports.

Under able expertise and steadfast leadership, the Indian Navy brought back many Indians from the port towns to Djibouti, from where they were taken to India. Even more, as some progress took shape, it was Prime Minister Modi's diplomacy that gave wings to the operation. Sushma Swaraj recalled how, by bringing a personal touch to diplomacy,

Prime Minister Modi made a prompt and direct call to the Saudi king in Riyadh, with whom he shared an excellent rapport, requesting a safe passage and support for the evacuations. The support was critical since the Saudis were then controlling the airspace over Yemen. While the Saudi king acknowledged India's request as too important to be ignored, he also expressed his inability to completely halt the bombings. However, he did agree to halt the bombings between 9.00 a.m. and 11.00 a.m. for a week. Subsequently, the Yemenis were requested to open the airport in Sanaa for evacuation.

Following intense negotiations, India was provided a window to launch the evacuation operations in Sanaa. India would fly in two to three empty aircraft from Djibouti, and they would be invariably packed on their way back from Sanaa. The team at Djibouti had to coordinate with the incoming flights from India. They arranged the landing permits, parking space, fuel, and other services for the flights in Djibouti and got the flying permits from the Saudis and landing approvals from the Houthi rebels in Sanaa. And, finally, the entire process was repeated in reverse for the return journey.

Interestingly, to ensure that things were under control, General Singh and Ambassador Verma flew to Sanaa from Djibouti no less than five times on an Air India flight, despite being advised against taking such risks. During one such visit, the short window for the air evacuation was closed for that particular day, so the Air India flight could not return. This meant that General Singh was stranded in the Yemeni capital and could not make it back to Djibouti. General Singh, accompanied by an Indian Foreign Service officer, Anjani Kumar, drove to Sheba Hotel (formerly Taj Sheba Hotel) on

Ali Abdolmoghni Road in the city. On the way there, they witnessed the destruction caused by the bombings everywhere. 'That night, we could hear the sound of bombings in the dead of night. It was an eerie feeling,' Kumar said, remembering those moments.

Notably, India received laudable support from the Bohra community in Sanaa, whose representatives were present every time General Singh flew in. More so, leaders of the community supported the government with proper information and local guidance, which was critical to the success of the operation.

About a hundred flights were handled in nine days at the Djibouti airport. At one point, there were eight Indian aircraft on the tarmac! Till mid-April, Operation Raahat evacuated 6,688 people—including 4,741 Indians and 1,947 foreign nationals—by air (seven aircraft) and sea routes (five naval ships). The foreign nationals hailed from forty-eight countries, including the US, the UK, Australia, Germany, and even Pakistan. In fact, a foreign national from El Salvador reached out to General Singh for help when the latter had to stay in Sanaa for a night. The person was disturbed and said that he would be very grateful to Singh and the Indian government for their help and generosity. Singh assured him that he would be taken to Djibouti along with Indians the next day; the minister delivered on his promise.

Operation Sankat Mochan

A similar exercise, named Operation Sankat Mochan, was taken up in South Sudan, where the Modi-led government evacuated Indians. Violence erupted across Sudan in July 2016 after two warring factions came head-to-head. As the hostilities raged, normal services were disrupted, and the lives of the Indians stranded were in danger.

With directions from PM Modi, Operation Sankat Mochan was executed by the IAF and supervised by MoS General V.K. Singh. It involved meticulous planning in coordination with the local authorities (General Singh met the foreign minister of South Sudan, Deng Alor Kuol) as well as the support of the Indian peacekeeping contingent in the United Nations Mission in South Sudan. It was a well-executed mission. The evacuees were adequately informed of the movements, the landing timings of the IAF's C-17 aircraft, and evacuations so that they could be prepared. Overall, 153 Indians and two citizens of Nepal were evacuated from Juba, the capital of South Sudan. Still, there were some Indians who wanted to stay back for business reasons, and there were those who continued to live in South Sudan as they lived a little far from the danger zones.

Vande Bharat Mission

The Vande Bharat Mission, which evacuated Indians stranded in other countries after the outbreak of the COVID-19 pandemic, and operated flights under bilateral arrangements with twenty-six countries, had fourteen phases. As of October 2021, it had brought back 5,603,992 Indians via air; 3,987 via sea; and 502,151 via land, making it the biggest repatriation operation ever in the history of independent India. S. Jaishankar summarizes the evacuation mission perfectly: 'We brought back seven million people under Vande Bharat Mission from all over the world. No one has done that. It's the biggest evacuation and was done during Covid. That is [the] India that the world sees today.'[17]

It all began in late 2019, with multiple cases of a new, mysterious pneumonia outbreak around a seafood and live animal market in Wuhan, a Chinese city in the Hubei province with a population of eight million. Indian intelligence was privy to the hushed chatter emanating from the epicentre of the outbreak as early as December 2019, when the first COVID-19-related death was recorded. Over the next couple of months, the virus spread all over the world, choking global health systems. Consequently, new methods were devised to curtail it, including multiple travel bans and lockdowns. Due to these global lockdowns, Indians across the world found themselves at sea. Internal travel bans within the countries added to their woes. The government, via Embassies of India (EOIs) across the world, got in touch with stranded Indians and realized that the problem was much bigger than it seemed. Prime Minister Modi immediately directed government officials to closely monitor all developments.

On 17 January 2020, the government issued an advisory for travellers to China. Another such advisory was put out a week later. By the second half of January 2020, it was clear that the situation was rapidly deteriorating. Many Indian students, were studying medicine in Hubei province at that point in time. Naturally, amid allegations of China hiding the COVID-19 situation, the families of these students were very worried.

The Indian government swung into action and decided to evacuate its own citizens and citizens of other neighbouring countries from Hubei through three special flights. The first two evacuations, on 31 January and 1 February, happened on Air India flights, while the third, on 26 February, was done by an IAF C-17 Globemaster. A total of 766 people were evacuated, which included 718 Indians as well as 5 officials from the Embassy of India in Beijing, who had travelled to Wuhan to manage the evacuation process on the ground. The flights also carried forty-three foreign nationals belonging to seven different countries: twenty-three from Bangladesh, nine from the Maldives, two from Myanmar, one from South Africa, one from Madagascar, one from the US, and six Chinese citizens who were spouses and/or children of the Indians evacuated. On the last flight, the government also delivered 15 tonnes of medical aid with masks, gloves, and other medical equipment to the Hubei Charity Federation.

Upon landing in India, the evacuees were kept in government quarantine facilities at the Indian Army Camp in Manesar and the Indo-Tibetan Border Police (ITBP) Camp in Chhawla for two weeks and were tested for the virus twice. Only after all of them tested negative were they allowed to proceed to their respective homes—for two more weeks of self-isolation.

*

As the pandemic gripped the world and challenged nations, an evacuation plan prepared by senior officers in the Government of India (including top officers in our diplomatic and intelligence apparatus) was presented to Prime Minister Modi. On 21 April, the presentation gave a broad overview and a regional breakdown of Indians abroad, including the Gulf region, Russia, Central Asia, Southeast Asia, North America, South Asia, the Indian Ocean Region, Europe, Africa, and South America. More than 1.37 crore Indian passport holders were abroad at that point, and about 192,968 of them had compelling reasons to come back.

With the prime minister's approval, the Vande Bharat Mission began to take concrete shape. A list of best practices was put together, along with measures to be taken before arrival. The EOIs were directed to prioritize compelling cases and pre-arrange the passports based on domicile.

Simultaneously, SOPs were drawn up in consultation with the ministries of health and family welfare, civil aviation, and home affairs. State governments were also roped in through multiple video conferences. To facilitate the evacuation and coordinate efforts, teams of Ministry of External Affairs officers were constituted at the state and national levels.

On 5 May, the foreign secretary briefed state chief secretaries about the Vande Bharat Mission. A WhatsApp group was formed to bring state coordinators from the ministry, security agencies, Air India personnel, and the EOIs together. The nodal officers for the states coordinated the efforts between the governments, the ministry, and the EOIs abroad.

The mission commenced on 7 May. All the coordinating departments and agencies converged and adapted swiftly, just as the situation demanded. The demands for repatriation were being continuously assessed. The joint secretary (administration) coordinated the scheduling of the flights, their frequencies, and destinations from different countries.

The EOIs were collecting and updating the database of returning Indians every hour. Based on the demand, a consolidated list of flights was worked out. With the approval of the foreign secretary and the Ministry of External Affairs, the demand was forwarded to Air India. While the ministry engaged with Air India to decide on the aircraft requirements, the EOIs worked with local agencies for clearances and procedures.

As the operation began, a concentration of returnees built up in New Delhi and Mumbai. The Ministry of Civil Aviation, the Ministry of Home Affairs, the Bureau of Immigration, and state governments coordinated and developed a system of feeder flights. As the mission evolved, the Ministry of External Affairs also developed a portal called REPAT, which was designed to capture relevant data about returning Indians and categorize them. It made all the information related to their movements accessible in real-time. By the end of June 2020, the REPAT portal had over five lakh registrations.

*

Prime Minister Modi not only commended the lifesaving efforts of the crew and medical team that participated in the Wuhan evacuations but also held a telephonic conversation with an evacuee, Nizamur Rehman, and motivated him to combat the pandemic. The MBBS students who had spent some tense moments in Wuhan were extremely grateful to the Indian government for bringing Rehman and other evacuees back to India. One of them said, 'We were sixty students from Kashmir. We are spreading awareness in our region.'[18]

A similar effort was made to evacuate the thousands of Shia pilgrims from a makeshift camp in Qom, Iran. Since these pilgrims were in a place with a high incidence of the coronavirus, utmost caution had to be taken while evacuating them. The government sent teams from Delhi in advance to test them for the virus. Since Iranian systems were overwhelmed with internal crisis management, the Ministry of External Affairs had to take care of almost everything for the pilgrims. A six-member team from the Indian Council of Medical Research (ICMR) was also deputed to Tehran. Over the coming months, spanning over a year, the GOI spearheaded the largest repatriation exercise. A gargantuan task of bringing millions of Indians home when countries had closed their borders for travel.

Operation Samudra Setu

The primary objective of Operation Samudra Setu was to repatriate Indian citizens stranded in foreign countries (such as the Maldives, Sri Lanka, Iran, and the UAE) due to the COVID-19 pandemic and the subsequent lockdowns. The plan was to bring back stranded Indians via two navy ships, *INS Shardul* and *INS Jalashwa*. The evacuation happened in close coordination with the Iran Navy, the Islamic Revolutionary Guard Corps Navy, the Governor's office, etc. Operation Samudra Setu was launched on 5 May 2020 by the Indian Navy, and it lasted for nearly two months.

The success of the operation was also attributed to the cooperation of and coordination with foreign governments. The Indian Navy worked closely with authorities in the respective countries to facilitate the smooth evacuation process. Many Indian citizens were stranded in foreign lands without adequate resources or support. The operation provided a lifeline for these individuals to return to their homeland during a time of global crisis. The Indian Navy personnel worked tirelessly to ensure that the evacuation process was carried out smoothly and efficiently. They conducted medical screenings of evacuees, provided necessary supplies onboard, and ensured adherence to COVID-19 protocols.

Operation Samudra Setu left a lasting legacy, highlighting the Indian Navy's capabilities in conducting complex, humanitarian operations overseas. It also underlined the government's commitment to the well-being of its citizens, both within the country and abroad.

Operation Ganga

During the COVID-19 phase, we saw Indians returning home safely and were also witnesses to a country-wide lockdown. As shared earlier, it was right after this phase of lockdown that I began researching evacuations and got into a conversation with many officers of the GOI. However, it was the Ukraine war and the evacuation of Indian students from there that brought forth some remarkable insights for me as a researcher.

In February 2022, even as the world was slowly stepping out of the pandemic's challenges, Russia invaded Ukraine over a long-brewing issue over the latter's inclination to join the North Atlantic Treaty Organization (NATO) and its generally pro-Western stance on many issues. The Government of India was quick to assess the deteriorating situation and began tracing all Indians across Ukraine through its embassy's process. This was done as a safe measure in case things escalated. And they did escalate. Russia continued to amass troops at the border. Sniffing danger, foreign nationals slowly began to leave Ukraine. The US classified Ukraine as a 'Level 4: Do Not Travel' category, stating that this was done due to the continued threat of Russian military action.

On 23 January 2022, the US Department of State authorized the voluntary departure of the US's directly hired employees and ordered the departure of eligible family members from its embassy in Kyiv. American personnel and citizens were advised to depart using commercial or other privately available transportation options. The State Department issued an advisory warning, which made it clear that the US would not be able to evacuate its citizens in the event of Russian military action anywhere in Ukraine. The US government also reiterated its inability to provide emergency services to its citizens in these regions.

Seen against this backdrop, what India achieved over those two weeks after the war began was a special feat. The mission to evacuate its citizens from Ukraine through coordinated efforts, unwavering determination, and international cooperation was paramount. There were thousands of Indian nationals stranded there, and to safely repatriate them amidst a volatile situation was a herculean task. The Indian government was tracking all developments through multiple channels, including intelligence and diplomatic. The Eurasia desk of the Ministry of External Affairs was in touch with the Indian ambassador in Ukraine, and other channels were bringing in more information that could help the Indian cause. The Indian embassy in Kyiv was small, but it managed the presence of over 25,000 Indians in Ukraine, of whom a majority were students. While the EOI continually monitored the media and the evolving situation on the ground, more intelligence and information were collated from various quarters and multiple sources.

On 20 February, Russia made an announcement with regard to the Luhansk and Donetsk regions, and it became clear that the situation would soon escalate into a full-blown war. Notably, India was also operating under an air-bubble arrangement with Ukraine. This meant that the number of flights in and out of Ukraine was limited. To augment it, the Ministry of Civil Aviation arranged for more flights to facilitate students who wanted to move out of the country. However, an Air India flight, sent to bring back Indians from Ukraine, had to turn back from the Iranian airspace because Russia attacked Ukraine on February 22.

Overnight, everything changed. Roads were blocked and movements restricted as Ukraine woke up to blasts all over the country in the early hours of the morning. Many Ukrainians began moving westwards to the land borders of Poland, Romania, Hungary, and Slovakia. Long lines of cars began piling up near the borders. Amidst all of this, Indian students were stranded.

Among the number of Indians in Ukraine, a large majority of them were students who had travelled there for medical education. These students mostly belonged to middle-class families and had taken out loans to study there. Over the years, the number of Indian students studying in Ukraine had kept increasing. Due to lack of clarity from the Ukrainian government and their respective universities on the way ahead, these students were in a dilemma. Before the war began, there were some options available. Notably, many students had also booked air tickets to travel out of the country. However, with the war having begun, the Ukrainian airspace was shut down.

The Modi government was already in action mode for the last few weeks, but before anyone realized it, multiple war fronts had opened in Ukraine. Under Prime Minister Modi's leadership, the government decided to launch an evacuation mission called Operation Ganga with a two-pronged strategy and adopt the 'Whole of Government' and 'All of Society' approach for evacuations. It began with a proactive stance from the prime minister, who involved multiple ministries in coordinated efforts. Special envoys were sent to countries neighbouring Ukraine—Poland, Hungary, Slovakia, and Romania. Four union ministers—Hardeep Singh Puri, Jyotiraditya Scindia, Kiren Rijiju, and General V.K. Singh (retired)—were Modi's special envoys.

*

Puri was in Guwahati, Assam, for a conference. After a hectic day, he had retired to bed, when, around 11.30 p.m., he received a call from the Prime Minister's Office. He was informed that the prime minister had deployed him as one of his envoys. Similarly, Kiren Rijiju was at his Delhi home when, around midnight, he received a call from Prime Minister Modi. In no time, all arrangements were made. The prime minister held two meetings the following day, and by evening, the ministers were ready to command their respective missions. They were helped with all the fine details related to the situation (border reports and challenges) and other local support, and everything that the embassy could do was aligned.

Every morning, Prime Minister Modi would take a brief on the developments related to evacuations before taking on other issues of the day. Since it was election season, he would have a meeting before he began campaigning and would take another follow-up meeting later in the day. A two-pronged plan was worked out, wherein Indians would first be moved via land to Ukraine's neighbouring countries—Poland, Romania, Hungary, Slovakia, and Moldova—from where they would be flown back to India. As many as forty-seven officers, including Russian-speaking, were moved from different places to coordinate the evacuation efforts. It was decided that the students and the other Indians would be shifted westwards through all available means.

To facilitate the process, the EOI Kyiv got in touch with student contractors/agents to facilitate admissions in Ukraine. The system was well in place. For instance, Dr. Masroor, a former MBBS student in Ukraine, had become a contractor after his studies. In 2014, he had seen the tragedies of the war and shifted base to the western side of the country. Like him, there were about twenty prominent agents who were active throughout the country, with their own independent set-ups. The embassy began coordinating with these agents.

Since a very large number of Ukrainians began moving westwards, Ukraine's largest land border to the west, Poland, was blocked; there was no way to cross it easily. Those who resided closer to the western borders were first asked to move. It was hoped that even if they could not get across it, they would at least get a fair idea of how the situation was on the ground, and they could even come back to their hostels if the situation compelled them to do so.

The Indian government simultaneously mobilized more officers to strengthen the EOIs in the neighbouring countries. Indian diplomats moved to the border towns of Romania, Hungary, Slovakia, and Poland and set up base camps there to coordinate the inflow of Indians. These base camps were also coordinating with the local government and their embassies and relaying real-time information to Delhi. At the same time, S. Jaishankar spoke with foreign ministers of the neighbouring countries, who warmly responded to India's requests. All of these carefully calibrated efforts were being closely looked into by the country's top leadership, including Prime Minister Modi.

PM Modi also spoke with the leadership of the neighbouring countries to rally their support. It was a consequence of his standing in international geopolitics and his efforts to establish long-lasting relations with foreign governments that Indian efforts received all the necessary support. It was also, in fact, largely a consequence of the personal diplomacy of the prime minister that helped our case. For instance, while speaking with the prime minister of Poland, Modi reminded him of the decades-old connection of Polish Jews with the Indian state of Jamnagar, Gujarat. This struck a special chord with the Poles. In fact, before this call, India had faced some hiccups in the evacuation process due to numerous factors. But, soon after, many of those challenges were streamlined, and the evacuations via Poland picked up pace.

PM Modi understood the anxieties of parents, whose children were caught in the crossfire. He directed people in the Ministry of External Affairs to open call centres that would inform parents of real-time developments. The EOI was asked to keep all communication channels open and also instructed that any information or directive had to be clear for everyone's understanding. Further, to assuage fears and anxieties, state governments were also directed to reach out to the parents.

People from the BJP leadership and the government reached out to individuals who could mobilize support for the neighbouring countries. For instance, the Bochasanwasi Akshar Purushottam Swaminarayan Sanstha (BAPS) leadership was contacted late at night on 27 February, and in the next few hours, many BAPS volunteers were mobilized who could bring resources and engage more people for evacuations. Similarly, Art of Living (AOL) was contacted for assistance. Notably, AOL founder, Sri Sri Ravi Shankar, spoke to anxious students and opened the doors of AOL's institutions in Europe to help in the efforts. Then, there was the International Society for Krishna Consciousness (ISKCON), which also has considerable presence in the region. Among other arrangements, ISKON volunteers offered hot food through a mobile van very close to the Ukraine–Poland border. Other organizations, such as the World Malayali Federation and Amma Maa Amritanandamayi's group, also came forward to help. In fact, the last evacuation via Poland was assisted by this organization.

The success of the operation was aptly summed up by S. Jaishankar in one of his parliamentary addresses: '*Speaker Sir, kuch din pehle ek videshi mantri aaye, unhone mujhe bahut garv se kaha ki mai do plane Ukraine se laya aur mujhse pucha, aapke plane kitne aaye? Aur wo hairaan tha jab maine kaha ninety planes aaye*' (Speaker Sir, a few days ago, a foreign minister visiting India proudly shared that he had brought back two planes from Ukraine and asked how many we had brought back. He was surprised when I said ninety planes).[19]

Pawan, an Indian businessman in Ukraine, who was in the thick of things in Sumy with the two officers from the EOI Kyiv, had this to say: 'All our efforts were yielding little. At one point, important people stopped picking up our calls. But then, thanks to Prime Minister Modi's intervention, everything was smoothened out. Permissions came in and we were allowed to move into Sumy and bring our students. In fact, if it was not for Prime Minister Modi, we would not have been able to rescue the Sumy students.'

Even more, India's efforts helped to evacuate people of other nationalities out of Sumy. In fact, throughout the mission, across Ukraine, Indian efforts assisted other nationalities as well. For instance, there was a Pakistani student, Asma Shafique, who came on camera and thanked PM Modi and India for safe evacuations.[20]

Operation Devi Shakti

'It is time to end the forever war.' On 14 April 2021, US President Joe Biden announced the end of his nation's longest and costliest military conflict from the same spot in the White House where President George W. Bush had ordered the start of the war in Afghanistan after the 9/11 attacks, nearly two decades ago.

Biden declared that the gradual withdrawal of American troops would begin on 1 May and end on 11 September, on the twentieth anniversary of 9/11. As US troops began to withdraw, the Taliban began extending its control over the country's territories. Between the first week of July and the last week of August, the Taliban made rapid advances and brought many districts, including Herat, Ghazni, Kandahar, and Mazār-i-Sharīf, under their control.

Although the US's timeline for complete withdrawal was still around a month away, the Taliban's rapid advance made it necessary for foreign nations to act swiftly. Indian consulates in Kandahar, Jalalabad, and Herat were shut down, followed by Mazār-i-Sharīf in early August. The GoI had planned to evacuate all Indians by 31 August, primarily from Kabul, where the EOI was based. A few IAF flights were also scheduled for the same.

However, in the middle of August, the Taliban advanced fast and surrounded the city of Kabul, forcing Afghanistan's embattled President Ashraf Ghani to flee his country. The Taliban had overthrown the Afghan government, the national military was in disarray, and the leadership was gone. In the absence of any clear leadership, the Taliban ruled the roost.

Around noon, the decision to evacuate Kabul was taken. The question was: how would the evacuation be done? It was perhaps time to devise a well-crafted mechanism built on the foundation of old relationships.

Though many Indians, heeding the advisories issued, had already left the country, many still remained stranded in the war-torn country. However, ascertaining their number was a challenge. Unlike people of other nationalities, Indians did not generally register themselves in Afghanistan. To address this problem, a Google form link was circulated to calculate the number of Indians still in the country. Many were stuck in different locations. For instance, there were around 100 sherpas from the Darjeeling area who had congregated in a foreign embassy.

A 24x7 evacuation cell was established in Delhi's South Block, in which newly inducted officers of the foreign service were deputed for its everyday functioning. The cell began taking calls and built a database of Indians in Afghanistan. Operation Devi Shakti had begun. An officer recalls how the joint secretary and the ministry were up all night, negotiating the movements of cars, shelters, etc., while another officer in South Block, who had experience with aircraft routes and planning, was brought on board. Their dedicated efforts ensured that the first group of about thirty-five people, mostly staffers, was evacuated on the night of 16 August on an IAF plane. A much bigger group, with a total of 168 people (including 107 Indians), however, was not able to make it to the airport that day because the Taliban were not allowing Afghans to fly out easily, and a lot of checking was being done to prevent it. Hence, another flight had to be arranged.

From then on, however, reaching the airport became increasingly difficult. The Taliban were divided into factions, with conflicting interests such as areas under control, ethnic loyalties, etc. With the police and army overthrown, Taliban groups had also taken over all the checkpoints. Though control over the airport was being contested, it was still functional. It was, therefore, a major challenge to move people out of their safe zones to the airport from where they could be flown out. With remarkable efforts, which included a great deal of coordination and negotiation, about 140 Indians, including the staff of the EOI, its security, and a few media persons, were evacuated from Afghanistan on IAF flights. They reached Delhi via Jamnagar. With this, the EOI operations in the country were closed.

Around the same time, leaders of the Sikh community requested the government to evacuate Afghan Sikhs still stranded in Afghanistan. Subsequently, in a meeting of the Cabinet Committee on Security, Prime Minister Modi directed officials to ensure 'the safe evacuation of all Indians from Afghanistan and provide refuge to Afghan Sikhs and Hindus wanting to come to India.' Consequently, between 18 and 26 August, more evacuation flights were organized. Just how difficult the task was, and how commendable the effort, can be understood from the fact that all this was achieved without an Indian embassy in the country. A decision was, therefore, taken to station a small team at the airport in Kabul to facilitate the movement of people and help them with various processes before boarding flights to India.

In over five flights in the days that followed, Indians, Afghan Hindus, and Sikhs were brought back, along with three copies of the Guru Granth Sahib. On 22 August, the government evacuated 392 individuals from Kabul on three flights. This group consisted of twenty-four Afghan Sikhs, including two Afghan MPs—Narinder Singh Khalsa and Anarkali Kaur—and their families. The following day, the government brought back 146 citizens on four flights via Doha, where they had been brought on NATO and American aircraft.

Since the IAF C-17s could not fly over Pakistan, they had to take a detour to reach Afghanistan. Apart from the C-17s, the C-130J Super Hercules was also deployed by the government to evacuate stranded Indians from Kabul to Dushanbe and thereafter back to India. India managed to save its citizens and other nationals just in time, because on the evening of 26 August, the Hamid Karzai International Airport was attacked, killing close to 200 people.

Under Operation Devi Shakti, a total of 669 people were evacuated. This included 448 Indian nationals, 206 Afghans (including Hindu Sikh minority community members), and 15 people of other nationalities (Nepal, Lebanon, and Uganda) in seven flights (six flights operated between 16 to 25 August, and the last flight was on 10 December 2021). All Indian nationals who had sought repatriation to India were evacuated.

Even after Operation Devi Shakti, the Shiromani Gurudwara Parbandhak Committee (SGPC) continued to push for the evacuation of Sikhs still caught in Afghanistan. Sikhs, like Hindus, have been a small community in Afghanistan. Many of them felt that they were morally India's responsibility or at least hoped that India would extend a helping hand. Several members of the community had stayed back to take care of religious scriptures and were prepared to leave only if the Taliban allowed them to take these scriptures with them. For many reasons, including security of community members, Karte Parwan, an important gurudwara in Kabul, had become their home in those distressing times.

When Karte Parwan was attacked in June 2022, Manjinder Singh Sirsa, a BJP member and former president of the Delhi Sikh Gurudwara Management Committee, approached Home Minister Amit Shah. Since COVID-19 regulations were still in place, there were many other challenges to the evacuations that had to be considered. For instance, one officer remembers how tough it was to arrange a safe stay for the batch that was scheduled to depart from Afghanistan. A Sikh philanthropist had arranged for a flight, but the group could not reach the airport in time. So, they were accommodated in a hotel with great difficulty. Later, however, they were later evacuated after immense effort. A batch of fifty-five Afghan Sikhs and Hindus were brought back as recently as September 2022.

Reflecting on how Operation Devi Shakti was accomplished through years of carefully maintained relationships with the respective countries, S. Jaishankar recalls,

> It was as challenging as combining access to a secured American base that was on edge, surrounded by desperate Afghans and suspicious Taliban; of using Tajik rear support

for very rapid responses, of accessing Iranian airspace at short notice and of quietly utilizing Qatari facilitation! Now there were some of our nationals who were beneficiaries of seats in flights run by the US, France, UK or the Emirates and all these were very delicately negotiated. Now this might seem, even from my account, as exceptionally complicated logistics. But it was really more than that; behind it were years of relationships that really delivered at a time of need. Equally important, this represented the efficacy of a flexible and pragmatic Indian policy of multiple engagement.[21]

A Humane Touch

Notably, it is not just in helping out fellow Indians that the Modi government has shown a humane touch. It has reached out to countries in distress, too. From Operation Saahayta in 2019 wherein aid was sent to Mozambique after Cyclone Idai, to Operation Dost in 2023, in the aftermath of the devastating earthquakes in Turkey, India has earned global praise for its multiple humanitarian efforts.

Recalling the alacrity with which PM Modi responded, External Affairs Minister S. Jaishankar recalled in an interview, 'In a very short time he [PM Modi] wanted to know our thoughts ... I quickly consulted people in my own ministry, and literally within a few minutes, we were told—Ok, you got the go.' Notably, in less than forty-eight hours, teams were ready and sent to carry out Operation Dost in Turkey. This global engagement has also translated into a much broader rolc for Indian diplomats. Be it Operation Raahat, Sankat Mochan, the Vande Bharat Mission, or Operation Devi Shakti, officers of the Ministry of External Affairs have not shied away from taking on seemingly unimaginable missions and going the extra mile to bring Indians back to safety or help countries in need.

Given that it has become standard procedure for the government to help stranded Indians abroad, many take this support for granted as well. For instance, an Indian in Ukraine said, 'Of course, the Modi government has to help! We are Indians. It is natural that the prime minister pulls us out of trouble!' Such a sentiment of not just hope but also of certainty of help is a major departure from the past. We know of a time when the government was quite uninterested in intervening in such matters. Or there were occasions when the government swung into action only after a major public outcry and when other global players had done their job and exited from the playfield.

In the words of S. Jaishankar, 'What has now become an SOP [standard operating procedure] for the Delhi bureaucracy was initially a novel experience for all of us.'[22] The SOP also refers to a new kind of diplomacy under Prime Minister Modi that has left its mark on the nation's external dealings over the past decade. The shift in our approach is not limited only to evacuations from conflict zones; in fact, as mentioned earlier, India continues to position itself as a global power with a difference by conducting Human Assistance and Disaster Relief Operations (HADR).

Freedom from Sudan

More recently, the government conducted yet another daring evacuation mission in Sudan after rival factions got embroiled in a power conflict, leading to a civil war in April 2023. Khartoum (the capital of Sudan) was the epicentre of the raging conflict, and many of the over 3,000 Indians in the city were caught in the violence, including members of the Hakki Pikki tribe (bird-catchers and hunters from Karnataka). Taking full advantage of the critical and short time windows, Indians were moved from Khartoum and other parts of the war-ridden country to the city of Port

Sudan on the Red Sea. Apart from the port, the city also has an international airport. From Port Sudan, Indians were taken to Jeddah, from where they were flown back to India. To facilitate this circuitous movement, the Indian Navy's ships, such as *INS Teg* and *INS Sumedha*, alongside IAF aircraft C-130J and C-17, were pressed into service.

Similar to Operation Ganga, a high-level government meeting was chaired by Prime Minister Modi. His instructions were clear, and swift action followed. Press releases and advisories were sent out to ensure that every Indian took measures to remain safe so that they could be evacuated as soon as possible. The government had already begun negotiations and discussions on multiple fronts to secure a safe passage for the Indians out of Sudan. While the Ministry of External Affairs spoke with different stakeholders, including governments in the region and the UN Secretary-General, Minister of State V. Muraleedharan left for Jeddah (Saudi Arabia) to oversee the operation on the ground.

Remarkably, in a brave operation on 27–28 April 2023, the IAF rescued 121 personnel from a small airstrip in Wadi Sayyidan (about 40 km north of Khartoum). These included medical cases and a pregnant woman. With a degraded surface and no navigational approach or aids, the audacious mission was completed in approximately two-and-a-half hours. Others who had crossed over into Chad for safety were brought to safety as well.

The prime minister also met the evacuees of the Hakki Pikki tribe. Notably, it was the election season in Karnataka, and much before the polls, the Indians were brought home. Alongside this, India also helped other nationals, such as the French and the Nepalese. In fact, even as the British slowly moved out and Turkish planes were fired at, the Indian government successfully managed the evacuation of around

3,800 nationals. As they returned, slogans of '*Bharat Mata ki Jai*' filled the air. An evacuee remarked, '*Narendra Modi hai toh mumkin hai*. I love you, Indian Government!'[23]

Apart from these instances, there have been many more efforts by the Government of India, in which Indians have been rescued from tense situations. For example, India has emerged as a protector of the Indian Ocean. It has guarded the region from piracy and maintained a constantly strong presence. In recent times, it has worked on the overarching principle of Vasudhaiva Kutumbakam, that is, the world is one family, and lent support through all possible means. A recent case in point would be Operation Dost, which was launched after an earthquake devastated Turkey in 2023.

In 2024, following Prime Minister Modi's personal intervention, eight Indians, who had been sentenced to death in Qatar, escaped the noose. While it is obvious that their respective families were happy, the country too was reassured that the prime minister would go to any extent and manage what seemed impossible to secure the safety of his fellow Indians caught in distress.

Under Prime Minister Narendra Modi's leadership, India's evacuation operations have been characterized by efficiency, coordination, and a steadfast commitment to the safety of its citizens. The successful repatriation of Indian nationals from various parts of the world in challenging circumstances is a testament to the government's proactive approach and effective crisis management. When the Opposition continues to politicize matters and complicate situations, GoI stays focused on the task at hand. As India continues to navigate global challenges, the legacy of these evacuation efforts serves as a reminder of the nation's resilience and unwavering commitment to its citizens, no matter where they may be.

5

Global Diplomacy: Both Assertive and Humanitarian

'I would suggest your attention should be on Europe … Our purchases for the month would be less than what Europe does in an afternoon!'[1]

This stinging retort came from External Affairs Minister S. Jaishankar in response to a media query in April 2022. The question was asked in the context of energy purchases being made by India from Russia.

Who would have thought a decade ago that a senior minister in the union government would show the West the mirror in such a brutal manner! And who would have thought that the response would be taken so seriously and with so much delight by many across the world, that it would go viral!

The retort was not merely an answer to a question but an unequivocal assertion of India's right to make decisions that are driven, first and foremost, by its own national interests. That such a strong message should be delivered to the 'mighty' West was the icing on the cake. It demonstrated an attitudinal and mindset change; a change that began taking place soon after the Narendra Modi government assumed office in 2014.

In the case at hand, the context was the Russia–Ukraine war, and India was being asked by the Western powers to take sides—in effect, side with Ukraine, and stop buying energy from Russia. Jaishankar turned the tables on the West by saying, 'We buy some energy that is necessary for our energy security.'[2] Instead, a comparative analysis would make it clear India's position on the purchase. At the GLOBSEC forum in Slovakia in 2022, he further said, rubbing it in, 'Europe has to get out of the mindset that Europe's problems are the world's problems, but the world's problems are not Europe's problems.'

Nothing was preventing India from taking a similarly strong position on global matters in the past. Nothing, except, perhaps, the lack of self-confidence in our ruling leaders. Let us not forget that for decades, New Delhi had been tying itself up in knots by professing a policy of 'non-alignment', which was, by definition, neither here nor there. We did not want to say or do anything that would upset the superpowers or any other power, such as China. In the process, we even compromised with what we should have done in our national interests.

The Modi government changed that. In fact, even before becoming prime minister, during the election campaign, Modi made his intentions known on matters of foreign policy—that it would be assertive, and muscular if necessary. The government would do its best to maintain peace and cordiality with neighbours and the rest of the world but not by sacrificing its own interests.

This confidence, to some measure, also evolved over the years since 2014, because of India's rise as an economic power and a diplomatic power whose voice was being heard, respected, and supported by many other countries. Add to this the growing influence of the Indian diaspora in the West, a large part of which wholeheartedly backs Prime Minister Modi, and there was no way any country could brush aside India's stature.

To those who still harboured doubts, the Modi government demonstrated its resolve through actions. The position it has taken on the Russia–Ukraine conflict is one such example. It has consistently backed a peaceful resolution but refused to play the West's game of condemning Russia, its long-time friend and partner. Its military strikes inside Pakistan to weaken terrorist outfits that targeted India were an instance of converting words into action.

The Modi government's assertive diplomacy may have taken many observers by surprise, but it was in the making for a long time. Quite possibly, even as chief minister of Gujarat, he had begun to muse over the country's traditional response to foreign matters and what needed to be done to sharpen it. A clearer picture emerged over the years. Modi would extend an olive branch, even to India's most hostile neighbours, in a bid to course-correct their conduct towards this country. If it worked, well and good; if it did not, then the option of coercive action would be executed.

A New Experiment

Thus, for his oath-taking ceremony in 2014 as prime minister, he invited all the leaders of the South Asian Association for Regional Cooperation (SAARC). Eyebrows were raised, but to the surprise of many, all the leaders accepted the invitation and came.[3] This included Tibet's prime minister-in-exile, sending a clear message to China. As prime minister, Modi prioritized stronger and deeper ties with India's neighbours as well as those in Asia. The South Asia Satellite, named GSAT-9, was launched in May 2017 to benefit SAARC countries. It provides critical information on telemedicine, banking, television broadcasting, and education services. Equipped with state-of-the-art remote-sensing technology, the satellite is operated by the Indian Space Research Organisation (ISRO) on behalf of SAARC member countries.

At the same time, the prime minister reached out to the West and struck mutually beneficial arrangements; the International Solar Alliance (ISA) is only one such example.

The prime minister's foreign policy outreach towards hostile nations has been lucid. First, make sincere attempts to mend ties. If that fails, get assertive and stand one's ground. He made an impromptu, unofficial trip to Pakistan in 2015 to meet the then prime minister, Nawaz Sharif. Later, when Pakistan continued to play its old game, the ground strike and the air strike happened. Not without a provocation, however. Similarly, Modi visited China, parleyed with Chinese President Xi Jinping, and hosted Xi in India. But when Chinese troops turned aggressive along the borders, the Indian side, with clear instructions from the Modi government, paid them back in their coin.

It would not be an exaggeration to say that since coming to power, Modi has effected changes that have had a profound impact on the geopolitics of India, with the aim of giving India the global stature that it deserves. Policies such as Neighbourhood First and Act East underscore India's commitment to regional stability and engagement with the Indo-Pacific. Economic initiatives like Make in India have attracted investments, while India's leadership on climate change and multilateral forums has showcased its global ambitions and also demonstrated that it can lead by example.

Also, strengthening economic and strategic ties with countries such as Japan, Vietnam, and Indonesia has been a priority. Initiatives such as the India-Japan Special Strategic and Global Partnership and the trilateral India-Japan-US Malabar naval exercises underline India's growing role in the Indo-Pacific region.

*

Soon after his election, PM Modi took everyone by surprise with a flurry of visits abroad to shore up India's leverage and world status. There was a freshness in the way he approached the subject—many experts had earlier expressed doubts about his ability to handle tricky foreign relations. With his visits seen largely as supremely successful, all that the Opposition could manage was to question his frequent travels. They started making memes around the same without realizing that, on the ground, Indians approved the prime minister.

The fact that he saved time and money by travelling through the nights and using the days for meetings, as revealed by some of his close aides, made people back home, and even leaders abroad, shake their heads in admiration. He built a personal rapport with many world leaders, and while the Opposition was busy targeting him on petty things such as his accent or dressing style, PM Modi travelled the the world like a mighty Colossus, as Cassius said of Julius Caesar. This 'personal diplomacy' helped India in many instances, such as during the evacuations from Yemen when Modi called the Saudi king to assist in the exercise. Or, when he reminded Polish President Andrzej Duda about how the Jamnagar state helped Polish Jews during the Second World War. The conversation with President Duda resulted in Poland's assistance in the evacuation of Indians citizens in

Ukraine. It is such personal touches in diplomacy that have helped India achieve many breakthroughs.

Regardless, these trips enhanced the image of India across the world. Wherever Prime Minister Modi went, his schedule would be packed with multiple meetings with leaders of other countries. He would also attend public events and meetings to engage with the people—more precisely, with the Indian diaspora there. Modi has often said that every *pravasi* Bharatiya is a national ambassador who can act as a messenger of India's glory. And, why not? According to the United Nations Department of Economic and Social Affairs (UNDESA) report in 2020, 18 million Indians live outside their country of birth, distributed across several major countries of destination, including the UAE (3.5 million), the US (2.7 million), and Saudi Arabia (2.5 million), among others. Other countries hosting large numbers of migrants from India include Australia, Canada, Kuwait, Oman, Pakistan, Qatar, the UK, and Northern Ireland.

The Power of Diaspora

Since taking office in 2014, Prime Minister Modi has prioritized the Indian diaspora like no prime minister has ever done. He was the first to see the diaspora as 'allies, benefactors, and unofficial ambassadors' and tapped into its enormous potential. He built a personal rapport with hundreds of diaspora organizations abroad. Moving beyond the party-loyalist outfits, such as Friends of BJP, he addressed massive crowds of the Indian diaspora, and such events included NRIs and PIOs from all quarters. These interactions built a sense of confidence and trust among Indians abroad. They not only felt wanted and appreciated by India but also got the assurance that India stood by them. This was a far cry from previous governments, some of whose leaders had not only ignored the Indian diaspora but even at times held them in contempt, accusing them of 'betraying' India—the NRIs were derisively referred to as 'not required in India'.[4]

The diaspora responded in equal measure to Prime Minister Modi's appreciation. From Madison Square Garden in New York and Westminster Central Hall in London to the Qudos Bank Arena in Sydney, Modi received frenzied receptions from ethnic Indians. It is a feat unmatched in scale by any politician or head of government in the twenty-first century.

Right from the beginning, Modi understood the linkage between the country's foreign policy and the Indian diaspora. Manoj Ladwa and Bharat Barai, who have known the prime minister for decades, say,

> His international diplomacy has won many friends and secured precious relationships. He has often acted in ways that are different from traditional means. But what may appear at times to be unconventional methods of engagement and diplomacy with the international community have also enabled an unparalleled rise in India's reputation as a predictable and dependable partner.[5]

Naturally, this interaction with the Indian diaspora has developed into a great symbiotic relationship.

From the 1970s until the 1990s, most Indians who went abroad did so as a consequence of the scarcity of professional avenues that existed in India. They would contribute to the large brain drain that the country witnessed. But this has changed greatly since Modi took office. Apart from being called India's global ambassadors, the diaspora has become an important part of Indian foreign policy initiatives; often, the diaspora leaders engage with local embassies and are an intrinsic part of Government of India events. This relationship extends beyond the political; it finds resonance in socioeconomic aspects as well. I remember speaking to a few relatives who are settled in the US and have flourished over the years. They often argued that they had little connection with the temples, social institutions, and, in general, the Indian diaspora group. But this changed dramatically in the last ten years. Hence, be it the 'Howdy Modi' event or the reception Prime Minister Modi received in Australia, the diaspora interacts and engages actively with Modi and India.

Sushma Swaraj, who served as the external affairs minister from May 2014 to May 2019, used social media effectively to engage with Indians and the diaspora. It was something that really attracted the youngsters. She was speaking to them from a platform they were comfortable in. One of her major achievements was the adoption of International Yoga Day by the United Nations. She played a pivotal role in garnering support from various countries for Prime Minister Modi's initiative, which led to the United Nations declaring June 21 as International Yoga Day.

Swaraj's tenure also exemplified soft diplomacy at its best. One example of effective crisis management was during the earthquake in Nepal in 2015, when India provided significant assistance and relief efforts to the affected nation. Swaraj worked towards deepening India's strategic partnerships with countries such as the US, Japan, and Israel. These efforts were aimed at bolstering India's position on the global stage and enhancing cooperation in areas such as defence, technology, and counter-terrorism.

She also focused on improving India's relations with African nations. This led to the hosting of the India-Africa Forum Summit in 2015, which aimed to boost cooperation in various sectors, such as trade, investment, and technology transfer. Sushma Swaraj worked to streamline and improve

India's consular services, making it easier for Indian citizens abroad to access services such as passport and visa-related matters. This included simplifying procedures and enhancing the efficiency of the Ministry of External Affairs' responses to citizens' concerns. Her tenure as external affairs minister was marked by proactive diplomacy, a focus on citizen-centric services, and efforts to elevate India's standing in the global arena.

A New Confidence

As India was making its mark on the global stage, in parallel, an interesting development was taking place on the sidelines: international relations as a subject was increasingly being chosen as a postgraduate degree in India. The number of students taking an interest in geopolitics and the rise of young participants at the Raisina Dialogue (organized by the Observer Research Foundation) is a case in point. The dialogue is organized in partnership with the Ministry of External Affairs and brings global leaders, academics, and policy professionals together every year in a grand way. Alongside, the ORF curates other events, meetings, etc., bringing young professionals from many nationalities together in a cohort who discuss global issues for about two weeks. Over the years, I have seen how Raisina Dialogue has become the face of non-official foreign policy conversations in India through the relentless hard work of Dr Samir Saran and his team.

It was in a podcast recently, where an international relations academic shared how Prime Minister Modi has made the study of international relations 'cool and accessible'. Before him, international relations as a subject was treated as a topic that belonged to a select few. One could argue that this was the face of the Indian policy set-up for decades before Modi.

I remember my visit to Slovenia in 2022, when I atteneded the Young Bled Strategic Forum. The forum brings together leaders from across Europe, but it was a pleasant surprise to see the Eastern European leadership huddling around the very scenic Lake Bled to discuss matters of key importance. I heard Ukrainian President Volodymyr Zelensky speak on the Russia–Ukraine war, as he pleaded for more funding to take on the Russians. Interestingly, there were many other opinions about the war as well. I was working on an essay on evacuations back then, and it was interesting to hear the perspectives of not just Hungary, Poland, Romania, Slovakia, and Moldova, but also what Armenia or Georgia thought about Europe's place in the world.

The forum was a great exposure, and I managed to do some long reading sessions at the bank of Lake Bled! However, there was something more interesting that I found out from the locals.

Slovenia is not a very populated country. Formerly a part of erstwhile Yugoslavia, it attained independence in 1991. Interestingly, in this seemingly remote and idyllic part of the world, Josip Broz Tito (a communist Yugoslav leader and President of Yugoslavia) had a villa, where he hosted some world leaders. Indira Gandhi had once been a guest there. This was news to me.

It was the local Slovenians who taught me about my own leader's past. It is well understood that Indira Gandhi's foreign policy stance was moving from Nehru's idealism towards some pragmatism. But international relations then and later remained the field of a select few for decades. Only a select group would be privy to gossip. Only the coterie would know about where the world is perhaps headed and who would be the mover and shaker. Consider it from the point of view of someone who literally believes, acts, and works in the domain where the world is their oyster. Only that select group of people would care about foreign policy. Because most others, in this case Indians, would hardly get out of the battle for daily bread. This is, perhaps, why meetings such as the ones in Slovenia were unknown to most Indians.

Another thing that PM Modi has done, then, is make international relations and foreign policy attractive for many. There is a steep rise in interest. Many more students want to study geopolitics and make an impact by playing on the global geopolitical scale. Many chose foreign service; yet many more contribute in the thinktank space, Track 1.5 and Track 2 dialogues. A rising number of Indians are also participating in international young leaders' conferences and workshops. All of this was visibly little until PM Modi took office. Or, limited to a select few. In this thread, I think it will be interesting to recollect how PM Modi, after stepping out of Gujarat politics in the 1990s, made Delhi (and Panchkula) his base. It was this tenure before he stepped up as the chief minister of Gujarat that he had the opportunity to visit as many as forty countries. It was his experience of working with the diaspora and understanding of where India stands that perhaps helped him accomplish what he did.

In the last ten years, India has developed a newfound confidence in its diplomacy. It is unapologetic and keeps Indian interests right on top—and there is no compromise here. While we maintain a dignified stance based on our national interests during global conflicts, we also walk the humanitarian path by extending support through the supply of medicines and vaccines to many countries. *Vasudhaiva Kumtumbakam* is not just a slogan for the government today. Instead, it is an acting principle. Vasudhaiva Kutumbakam is a Sanskrit phrase that translates to 'The world is one family.' This ancient Indian philosophy emphasizes the idea of the entire world being interconnected and interdependent. It promotes the notion that all humans, regardless of nationality, race, religion, or culture are part of a single global family. Prime Minister Modi has adapted the ancient Indian humanistic philosophies to shape the country's modern diplomacy, for instance, by bringing Vasudhaiva Kutumbakam as the pivot.

In the context of India's foreign policy, it represents a guiding principle that underlines the country's commitment to peaceful coexistence, mutual respect, and cooperation with other nations. It suggests that India views the world not as a collection of isolated entities but as a unified community, where all nations share common interests and responsibilities.

The policy reflects India's approach to international relations, which seeks to promote dialogue, understanding, and collaboration among countries. It emphasizes the importance of diplomacy, non-violence, and inclusivity in dealing with global challenges and conflicts.

Vasudhaiva Kutumbakam is today often invoked by Indian leaders and policymakers to highlight the country's vision for a world where differences are celebrated and diversity is seen as a source of strength. It underscores India's desire to contribute positively to the global community, whether through peacekeeping efforts, developmental assistance, or by promoting cultural exchanges.

India and the G20

India has successfully hosted many international events over the decades, but the G20 summit held in 2023 showcased a new India—an India that had truly arrived on the global stage. Confident but not arrogant; assured of its stature but humble in its dealing with others; leading from the front but also letting others register their presence.

The G20 event provided India with a platform to showcase its economic achievements, cultural richness, and diplomatic engagement to the world. As the world's largest democracy and a growing economic powerhouse, India's leadership of the G20 underscored its commitment to international cooperation, sustainable development, and shaping a more inclusive global order. While the summit culminated in a grand function held in New Delhi, sectoral and thematic functions connected with the G20 event were organized in different parts of the country, thus allowing delegates to get a glimpse of India's diversity and connecting Indians from all across the country to this historic event.

The G20 summit is a platform where the world's largest economies converge to discuss pressing global issues, ranging from economic growth and financial stability to climate change and sustainable development. In this context, India's position as the host country highlighted its commitment to fostering dialogue and collaboration among nations to address shared challenges.

India's GDP growth has consistently outpaced many other major economies, making it a crucial driver of global economic expansion. By hosting the G20, India took the opportunity to showcase its economic achievements, reforms, and investment potential to a global audience. This would help attract greater foreign investments, promote trade ties, and strengthen cultural and economic partnerships with other G20 members.

Furthermore, India's vibrant cultural heritage and diversity provided a unique backdrop for the G20 summit. From its ancient traditions to its modern innovations, India presents a rich tapestry of culture, art, and history. As the host, India offered delegates a slice of its cultural landscape through various events, performances, and exhibitions, promoting cultural exchange and understanding among nations.

On the diplomatic front, India's role as the G20 host allowed it to engage with a diverse group of nations on a wide range of issues. Through bilateral meetings and discussions during the summit, India could strengthen its diplomatic ties, promote its foreign policy objectives, and contribute to shaping the global agenda. It is this diplomatic engagements that are crucial for India as it seeks to play a more assertive role in international affairs and advance its strategic interests.

Moreover, India's hosting of the G20 reflected the changing dynamics of global power. With traditional powers facing challenges and emerging economies gaining prominence, India is becoming a strong voice in shaping global policies. India's leadership of the G20 signifies a shift towards a more multipolar world order where diverse perspectives and voices are valued in global decision-making processes.

In 2024, the foreign policy also shows a reflection of *Panch Pran,* which the prime minister spoke about in his Independence Day speech in August 2022. Although I discuss the Panch Pran pledges in detail later, it is pertinent to bring them here as well. The first pledge is to work towards the goal of a developed India. Then it asks us to remove all traces of the colonial mindset and take pride in our roots. While one may argue about how much of this has been understood and acted upon by the people of India today, it is interesting to note how the government itself is acting upon it, and encouraging others to follow suit.

Mandala Theory in Geopolitics

While we are on this subject, it would be useful to mention S. Jaishankar's book *Why Bharat Matters*. It's an important work, considering that it explains the path that the country's foreign policy has adopted. The book also explores the Mandala Theory—a concept in psychology that was developed by Carl Jung, a Swiss psychiatrist and psychoanalyst. It is derived from the word 'mandala', a geometric pattern that represents the universe in Hindu and Buddhist symbolism.

In Jungian psychology, the Mandala Theory is used to understand the process of individuation, which is the development of the self. The Mandala Theory is also used in a broader sense in spiritual practices as a tool for meditation, mindfulness, and achieving a sense of unity with the cosmos. According to Jung, the Mandala symbolizes the process of integrating the various elements of the unconscious and conscious selves. This includes integrating the conscious with the unconscious, the personal with the collective, and the masculine with the feminine.

But how is the Mandala Theory relevant to the practice of international relations by India? It tells us that we no longer have to depend on foreign scholars and theorists to understand and develop India's foreign policy. Instead, we have our own scholarly understanding of global politics, which we can use to our advantage.

Under Prime Minister Modi's leadership, India has managed to deepen its relations with Japan, Australia, the US, the UK, and other powers. In West Asia (or the Middle East), we have built independent, economically rooted relations with the powers in that region. India has managed to develop a strong footing in the neighbourhood as well. At the Raisina Dialogue 2024 recently, I got into a conversation with a group of young diplomats and academics. While many things were being discussed, at some point the talk converged on a conversation about Modi's foreign policy and where India stands on numerous issues. The discussion ended fairly well, and the consensus was that Modi's foreign policy is assertive; however, we play in the international domain with a functional set of principles. We play by the rules and want peaceful coexistence across the world, but we do not tolerate injustice and unprovoked aggression against our sovereignty. The principle largely emanates from our Hindu understanding of the world.

Managing Global Powers and Sentiments

In the roughly first sixty-five years of Independence, the Indian government sought to balance its relations with global powers, such as the USSR and the US. The Soviet Union, however, collapsed around the same time when India opened its markets for global trade. The non-aligned nations, which were fairly populous and flag-bearers of the global economy for about 1,800 years before the colonizers came in, were left in poverty and without adequate support. During the 1970s, India was, for all practical purposes, aligned with the Soviet Union, considering its strategic interests and the global power play. But with the changed scenario, the country needed to tweak its game plan.

From Nehruvian idealism to a level of pragmatism, India has now shifted towards unapologetic pragmatism alongside the philosophy of Vasudhaiva Kutumbakam which Prime Minister Modi has brought to the fore. It is indeed a consequence of this that Indian foreign policy now stands for global peace, the collective development of the world, and India's deserved place on the global geopolitical map.

However, it is interesting to recall how this change happened. Before Modi took office, India's place in the world was shaky. Around 2010, India became particularly infamous for corruption and red-tapism, and the country had a poor reputation on issues of internal and external security. Indian interests were, for some reason, hyphenated with Pakistan. Terrorism and extremism had plagued normal functioning within the country, and these troubles echoed across the world.

It was against this backdrop that Modi stepped out to build relationships. Take, for instance, his South Asian plan, and then the East Asian outreach. As prime minister, through his unique personal diplomacy, he has achieved some unimaginable things in West Asia, for instance, the BAPS temple in Abu Dhabi or the evacuation of not just Indians but people from other nationalities from war-like situations in the region.

In 2019, I was working in the Haryana chief minister's office. Manohar Lal Khattar, who was then the chief minister, had made a name for himself in the state by bringing about some positive changes. For example, transparency in government job selections, removing interviews (and consequently, discretion) from the selection process in many jobs, making the transfer process more open, etc. While working and learning through policy in action and politics on the ground, I got an opportunity to attend a conference in Hamburg, Germany.

The conference revolved around the idea of global governance and brought together over fifty accomplished young individuals from more than forty nationalities. Thus, there were diplomats, professionals working in the energy sector, media personnel from West Asia, civil servants working for international NGOs, and politicians in the making.

Add to the experience the opportunity to meet sharp-minded people in Europe who were either just travelling through or had parked their camps in Berlin or Hamburg. It was an intellectually stimulating environment, perhaps parallel to what Subhas Chandra Bose saw in the 1940s. Anyway, one thing that particularly stood out for a nationalist (I would define myself as such) was the lack of conversation around India and Asia. Or, the European obsession with itself. Almost all sessions pertained to European powers, their conflicts, and their interests. Of course, this had to have the America-centric view of the world, and so was it.

A lot has changed five years down the line. While in 2019, Prime Minister Modi was powerful and admired, he was perhaps not yet considered as important as, say, Vladimir Putin or Donald Trump, on the international stage.

What happened, one may ask? Well, a lot.

In 2020, the world was taken down by the COVID-19 pandemic. Global health systems were overwhelmed by the black swan event. People across the world were dying, and major powers whom the world looked up to for help, acted in benign self-interest. Hence, smaller countries that had little say in the geopolitical table were left orphaned.

What India did in those moments of acute crisis is that it became a helping brother to many nations and their citizens across the world. In line with the principle of Vasudhaiva Kutumbakam, India kicked off what came to be called 'Vaccine Diplomacy'. When global production was strained, Indian drug manufacturing companies, notably Bharat Biotech and Serum Institute of India, aided by the swift clearances that the proactive Government of India gave, made available home-grown vaccines. Not only were millions of people in the country vaccinated—in what was one of the world's biggest vaccination drives—but India also exported the vaccines to needy countries. Thus, millions across the globe were vaccinated by Covaxin and Covishield.

Not just that, over a short period, it also offered telemedicine services, personal protection equipment, testing kits, etc., to other countries. Besides, it extended lines of credit and shared its experiences in combating the disease with neighbouring countries.

In 2022, when the world was still reeling under COVID-19 pressures, Russia invaded Ukraine. After the collapse of the USSR, Russia became a centre that commanded the most power and clout in the region. Meanwhile, through the efforts of NATO and the EU, the American hold on global supremacy kept getting stronger, and the expansion of its influence came closer to the Russian borders. While a conflict had been simmering in Ukraine since 2014 (Russian annexation of Crimea), Russian President Putin was clear about the fact that Ukraine and Russia shared a civilizational history and that the eastward expansion of NATO was a no-go. Ukraine is the red line!

However, as the situation unfolded, Russian missiles attacked Ukraine, targeting major cities. As the country turned into a war zone, India also carried out a remarkable operation (details in chapter 4) and brought its nationals back into the country under the mission named Operation Ganga.

However, in hindsight, it is important to reflect on the position that Prime Minister Modi was in during the conflict. He was one of the few leaders, perhaps the only one, who could effectively initiate a conversation between President Putin and President Zelensky. India was able to negotiate a window and temporarily stop the war in Sumy (Ukraine) on humanitarian grounds—it moved buses arranged by Indian diplomats in Ukraine and got over 600 Indians and about the same number of people from other nationalities out.

Of course, many other factors were at play. But, India's position and reasoning gave it a fair advantage. In a meeting with President Putin, Prime Minister Modi emphasized that dialogue and diplomacy were the way forward. He said, 'Today's era is not an era of war.'

In his historic address to the US Congress in June 2023, PM Modi said that the war in Ukraine involved major powers and that the consequences were severe. 'As I have said, this is not an era of war. It is of dialogue and diplomacy,' he remarked. Earlier, in a joint press conference with US President Joe Biden at the White House after their talks, Modi reiterated that India was ready to contribute in any manner to restore peace. As recently as March 2024, the prime minister tweeted the following: '[Had] a good conversation with President Zelensky on strengthening the India-Ukraine partnership. Conveyed India's consistent support for all efforts for peace and bringing an early end to the ongoing conflict. India will continue to provide humanitarian assistance guided by our people-centric approach.'[6]

India's Expanding Influence

These developments reflect positively on our position in the world. For instance, in 2024, when one speaks about or represents India at an international conference, one finds to one's delight that the image of the nation has remarkably altered. India is spoken about not just as the most populous and largest democracy in the world but also with the respect that it deserves. We are an important seat on any global table. We are a stable democracy, a rising economy, and we represent one-sixth of the world.

And, not merely this, the country understands its position on multiple matters and negotiates no more as someone else's pawn but in its self-interest. This was on full display for the world when India bought oil from Russia despite the West's sanctions, or when we argued for our interest in other theatres of the world.

In the United Nations and other international bodies, such as the G20, India has not only represented itself but also the collective voice of the Global South. Its foreign policy has evolved to become a bridge between the Global North and the Global South. From its rich history of anti-colonial struggles to its current role in shaping multilateral dialogues, India has been spearheading initiatives that promote inclusivity, sustainability, and mutual prosperity among developing nations. India actively engages in multilateral forums, robustly advocating the interests of those who deserve to be heard. Our country's emphasis on South-South cooperation has led to partnerships with countries across Africa, Latin America, and Asia, fostering trade, technology transfer, and capacity building. The International Solar Alliance (ISA), launched by India in collaboration with France, exemplifies the commitment to sustainable development and climate action. By promoting solar energy uptake among solar-rich countries, the ISA aims to address energy poverty and mitigate climate change, showcasing India's leadership in global environmental initiatives.

With this approach, India is also extending its zone of dominance. We are perhaps too obsessed with the issue of land borders. Pakistan, Nepal, China, and Bangladesh are our neighbours, but, if one considers maritime borders, countries such as Australia and South Africa are our neighbours too. In more recent years, there has been an appreciation of this reality, and it has resulted in India's increased presence in the Indian Ocean region.

India has emerged as the protector of the Indian Ocean, which is a critical maritime zone that connects the economies of Asia, Africa, and the Middle East. India's peninsula extends deep into the Indian Ocean, making it a natural geopolitical hub. Our location provides strategic advantages for trade, maritime security, and naval operations. Positioned between the energy-rich regions of the Middle East and the dynamic economies of Southeast Asia, India serves as a bridge between the East and West.

It also makes it a crucial transit point for global shipping routes. India, thus, is focussing a lot more on its relationships with countries in the Indian Ocean region, such as Sri Lanka, the Maldives, Mauritius, and the Seychelles, which are crucial for mutual security and economic partnerships; besides, there are cultural ties too.

Very recently, Indian presence in policing the ocean has been in the news across the world. Our maritime policing has led to the rescue of several crew members—Indian and of other nationalities—from the clutches of pirates.

In March 2024, the Indian Navy recaptured a ship from Somali pirates off the Indian coast and rescued the crew—who had been held captive for nearly three months—of the bulk carrier, *MV Ruen*. The operation was carried out by the

Indian warship *Kolkata*, and the Indian force compelled all thirty-five pirates to surrender.

In another incident, the Indian Navy freed an Iranian fishing vessel that had been hijacked by pirates and rescued its crew of twenty-three Pakistani nationals. The Indian ship, *INS Sumedha*, which intercepted the hijacked vessel, received backup support from a guided missile frigate, *INS Trishul*. The pirates were forced to surrender.

Hence, Indian foreign policy, both in spirit and action, has at the core Indian interests. What makes it work is that Prime Minister Modi prioritizes this approach. Geopolitics in action has multiple fronts and multiple cards to act with. To do so, Modi uses different strategies. He balances between the US, Russia, and China; keeps a friendly relationship with Southeast and East Asia; maintains stability in the Indian Ocean region; builds connections and protects our people in West Asia and Africa; increases trade with the West; procures resources from Latin America; and keeps the diaspora on high priority wherever they are.

6

New Narrative in Writing and Films

I was part of a panel discussion in Noida's Film City a few years ago. Those were the COVID-19 days. The session was tightly organized. The curator was the bestselling author and historian Vikram Sampath, and as always, with his honesty and charm, he brought many people together to discuss contemporary ideas and topics. I also moderated a discussion with authors Bhupendra Yadav, Union cabinet minister, and Ila Patnaik, economist. While the conversation with them on the rise of the BJP was interesting, the other discussion was more relevant to what I propose to delve into in this chapter.

The broad topic of the panel discussion was the retelling of Indian history. It was by no means a novel subject; it had been in discussion for the last couple of years. In fact, be it supporters of Prime Minister Narendra Modi or the usual critics, all had diverse but strong views on the matter. Vikram Sampath, who was curator of the program, himself had been the target of many malicious attacks for his bold espousal of truth.

However, sometime in the middle of the panel discussion, I found myself a little uncomfortable. Panel discussion as well as questions from the moderator were all concentrating towards the efforts of the authors, their work, and how they have, perhaps, battled with a publishing industry that was not willing to give them the space for their voice.

At one point, I was compelled to skip through the usual and added that we were all missing an important link. A link that, for long, many such conversations have avoided. Or we have, in some ways, taken it for granted. Writers, if serious, unknowingly put out a lot of themselves in between those lines they write. This is precisely why they are the sole owners of how remarkable or dull their work may be. It is in those minutes, hours, days, months, and years of life lived in the books they write. And not many are getting rich writing books. They are instead driven by another purpose. Perhaps, larger than themselves. It's their own story that is screaming to be told. Unless there is strong self-motivation, it can feel like a painful struggle. Until they have written back-to-back bestsellers—never mind if they have written good stuff—there is no way they can cause a commotion.

Regardless of this reality, the new-age India scholarship has found support and is consequently gaining acceptance because of one very important reason—Prime Minister Narendra Modi. And that is what I had to jump out and say in that panel discussion. Those who have seen the world of scholarship and nationalist literature since 2010 will be able to understand and even articulate this transition better.

Two Bad Influences

Modern Indian history, in its pre-Independence phase, has two key events that were fairly consequential in the post-1947 period. One would be Macaulay's Minute. In February 1835, British historian and politician, Thomas Babington Macaulay presented his *Minute on Indian Education.* Not only did he make a strong case for the promotion of English education to the 'natives' in India, but he also rubbished the learnings from the Indian local languages, infamously saying that a 'single shelf of a good European library was worth the whole native literature of India and Arabia'.[1]

Macaulay wished to cultivate a group of Indians who would support the so-called superiority of the English language and the wisdom derived from it so that they would rise from the 'inferior learning' from the Indian language texts. The British left India in 1947, but Macaulay's desire was carried forward by many Indians who had been brainwashed by his assertions. However, this was not just a matter of language; it had consequences for the cultural and civilizational history of India. For decades since Independence, the Indian Left-liberal ecosystem faithfully adhered to Macaulay's wishes, pushing the country's rich cultural legacy to the margins and designating anyone wishing to even talk of it—let alone revive it—as belonging to the fringe.

Macaulay's English education system, introduced during the colonial rule, therefore, had lasting adverse effects on Indian education after Independence. It eroded indigenous knowledge, exacerbated social inequalities, neglected vocational skills, hindered cultural development, and alienated students from their sociocultural realities.

The emphasis on English education led to the neglect, and sometimes active suppression, of traditional Indian languages, arts, and sciences. Subjects like philosophy, literature, and history, which were traditionally taught in vernacular languages, took a back seat. As a result, generations of Indians grew up disconnected from their own cultural roots and histories.

The English system favoured the urban elite and upper castes who had the means to access English-medium schools. Meanwhile, the majority of the population, especially in rural areas and among the lower castes, had limited access to quality education. This created a stark divide between the English-educated elite and the masses, perpetuating socioeconomic disparities.

Traditional Indian education systems placed a strong emphasis on skills such as carpentry, weaving, agriculture, and craftsmanship. However, Macaulay's system, with its focus on a narrow academic curriculum, sidelined these crucial skills. Consequently, generations of Indians were deprived of the opportunity to learn practical trades, leading to a shortage of skilled workers in various sectors.

Vernacular languages, which were the carriers of rich literary and cultural traditions, suffered neglect. This not only weakened linguistic diversity but also hindered the growth of regional literature, arts, and sciences.

The other important development was the rise of communism in India. Of course, there were other intellectual strands that emanated from V.D. Savarkar, Sri Aurobindo, etc. But in the phase immediately after Independence, these two—communism and Macaulayism—seemed to have had the greatest impact on post-1947 India.

The communist movement, with its intellectual and utopian inclinations, had caught the attention of many people across the world. It did have a considerable effect on our national movement, and the ideas that flowed from it spread into different domains of the Indian freedom movement. Since communism turned into a major political movement across the world and also due to the Cold War between the USSR and the USA, the implications became more evident in free India.

Although communist ideas failed to garner a pan-India following, they did result in political victories in some state elections. However, more than on politics, its impact on academia and the intelligentsia at large lasted longer. Hence, for decades after Independence, the nation was in the grip of socialist and communist ideas. While the economy was the pet area on which these ideas were experimented with, the academic output too reflected the influence in full measure. More books and research emerged that studiously ignored India's rich cultural legacy. Going one step further, they sought to dismiss our civilizational values as retrograde and not in keeping with what was commonly referred to as 'progressive' ideas. Thus, a generation of Indians who were apologetic about their own identities came to emerge.

All of this was happening under the political patronage of the Nehru–Gandhi family. Indeed, after Independence, it all began with Jawaharlal Nehru's tilt towards the narratives that the West-inspired writers dished out. His own socialist outlook, his apathy for Bharat's cultural ethos, and his positivity towards foreign invaders, such as the Mughals, meant that the academic and literary world followed in his footsteps; after all, being the tallest political figure and prime minister, he could make or break careers.

Examples of Resistance

Professor Kapil Kapoor (born 17 November 1940) is an Indian scholar of history, linguistics and literature and an authority on Indian intellectual traditions. He is the former pro-vice-chancellor of Jawaharlal Nehru University (JNU), New Delhi, and served as a professor at the Center for Linguistics and English and Center for Sanskrit Studies before retiring in 2005. He is the editor-in-chief of the 11-volume *Encyclopedia of Hinduism* published by Rupa in 2012. The Government of India awarded him with the Padma Bhushan in 2023. He shared, for example, how bureaucrats in Delhi would visit the temple in Chanakyapuri before heading to the office and specially request the priest for a light *tikka.* The babus would then wipe it off and head to work.

This echoes what happened in Bihar in 2007. The government's agriculture department head threatened to suspend an officer for sporting a *tilak* on his forehead when in office. The threatened official's colleagues, with all of them sporting the *tilak* to make a point, gathered in his support and created a ruckus in the secretariat. While this was just one incident, what is important is that it displayed a mindset that was anti-Indian to the core—less Hindu and anti-Sanatana.

While the Leftist tilt in academia and, consequently, in literature across different genres dominated popular writing, there was still—despite all odds—a parallel strand of nationalist literature being produced. The story of nationalist writers goes back to the Independence movement.

A cursory look at the documentation of Indian history reveals distinct schools of thought, including the Orientalist approach, the Cambridge school, the Marxian perspective, and the Subaltern school. In addition, the Hindutva approach is exemplified by Vinayak Damodar Savarkar, a prominent nationalist ideologue and a towering leader of the Indian freedom movement. The other school of thought then became the nationalist school. The nationalists were influenced by the

Indian history of glory and nationalism as expressed during the freedom struggle. It reflected confidence in the Indian civilization and praised the faith, philosophies, and culture of Bharat. But post-Independence Nehruvian secularism came down heavily on this approach.

From the late twentieth century to the present day, history writing in India has been embroiled in controversies, reflecting the complexities of a nation grappling with its past. The neglect of cultural and religious dimensions, economic determinism, political bias, and selective interpretations have collectively distorted the narrative, presenting an incomplete view of the complexities of Indian society.

Glimpses from Literature

This situation of Indic writing also resulted in a language bias. In the 1950s, movements across India arguing for linguistic divisions sprang up. As a consequence, select literature in select languages felt the burn. However, the spirit of nationalism was still preserved in vernacular languages. For instance, Hindi literature was enriched by the contributions of these patriotic writers, who used their literary prowess to uplift and unite the nation. Their writings serve as timeless reminders of the values of courage, sacrifice, and love for the motherland. Maithili Sharan Gupt, often referred to as the *Rashtra Kavi* (national poet), stands as a towering figure in Hindi literature. His poems, deeply rooted in Indian mythology and history, were infused with a fervent love for the motherland. Gupt's magnum opus, *Bharat-Bharati*, is a poetic tribute to India's cultural heritage and the spirit of nationalism. In this epic, he celebrates India's glorious past, paying homage to its heroes and martyrs while inspiring a sense of pride and patriotism among readers. His role in the *Chhayavaad* movement, with its focus on nature, spirituality, and love for the nation, cemented his place as a patriot-poet of Hindi literature.

Ramdhari Singh 'Dinkar' was another stalwart of Hindi literature whose works resonated with themes of patriotism and social consciousness. His powerful poems, marked by fiery rhetoric and deep emotion, became anthems of resistance during India's struggle for independence. His *Rashmirathi*, an epic poem based on the Mahabharata, is a stirring narrative of Karna's life, drawing parallels with the struggles of the common man and the quest for justice. In his famous poem, 'Singhasan Khaali Karo Ke Janata Aaati Hai', Dinkar exhorted people to rise against oppression and take charge of their destiny. The poem became a rallying cry during the anti-corruption movement in the 1970s, highlighting Dinkar's timeless relevance.

Subhadra Kumari Chauhan was a pioneer among Indian women poets, who left an indelible mark on Hindi literature with her nationalist poetry. Her most famous work, 'Jhansi Ki Rani', is a poignant tribute to the bravery and sacrifice of Rani Lakshmibai of Jhansi. Through this poem, Chauhan immortalized the courage of this iconic figure of the Indian freedom struggle, inspiring generations of Indians, especially women, to stand up against injustice.

An interesting case in point would be that of the celebrated writer, Raja Rao, who wrote in English. His books were a celebration of Indian thought and philosophy, and they also reflected an Indian-ness that became a hallmark of his writing. For example, *Kanthapura*, written well before Independence, has a strong Kannada influence. *The Serpent and the Rope* and *The Cat and Shakespeare* derive heavily from the Indian metaphysical school as well as our sacred texts. The influence of Sanskrit is evident in them. Raja Rao once famously said that although he wrote in English, he would not write like an Englishman. Unlike many Indian writers in English, who followed him, he remained rooted in Bharat. He 'Indianized' the English language in his novels so that it connected with the Indian audience while also finding appreciation globally.

The Role of Politics

Taking a long view of how nationalist narratives are taking shape in India today, 1991 becomes an inflection point. That phase marks an important change in the post-Independence history of India. The country was going through a churn. After Indira Gandhi's assassination in 1984, her son Rajiv Gandhi (her other son, Sanjay Gandhi, who was politically more active, was killed in an aeroplane accident) became the prime minister. He came with the image of a modernist, but that impression was dispelled after he capitulated to the hardliners in the Shah Bano case. He also tried to 'balance' things out with the opening of the locks on the Ayodhya temple. However, none of his actions could erase the impression that he was uncertain about how to take the nationalist view forward. He oscillated between one appeasement and another, ending up as a failure.

Moreover, five years into power, Rajiv Gandhi's popularity had diminished, and his government was marred by corruption and scandals. His exit was followed by a spell of political instability, which was broken with P.V. Narasimha Rao taking over as prime minister. Rao unleashed the historic economic reforms in 1991, turning on its head many so-called socialist policies and principles that governments had followed since Independence. He freed the private industry from government shackles, abolished the permit-quota raj, opened new sectors to private industry, and overhauled the trade policy so drastically that it had no resemblance to that of the past.

Rao's efforts had the most salutatory impact. The world took note, and investors got attracted to India. The journey of India's rise as an economic powerhouse began from there. His initiative also brought about a refreshing change in the old narrative, and Indians finally realized their potential and had the drive to achieve it. This change in mindset was an important addition to the nationalist cause.

But there was another development that impacted the country—the rise of the movement for the construction of the Ram Mandir in Ayodhya where the Babri mosque then stood. Organizations such as the Vishwa Hindu Parishad helmed the campaign, which caught national attention. The BJP became a part of the movement, with its senior leader L.K. Advani journeying across the country to drum up support for the cause of the temple (he had done it during Prime Minister V.P. Singh's tenure but was arrested when he reached Bihar, where Lalu Prasad Yadav was the chief minister). Now, the Ram Mandir movement had gathered pace, and Rao had to tackle it. The defining moment came when a large gathering of people at the then disputed site brought down the Babri structure in December 1992.

These events had a deep impact on many young impressionable minds and shaped the narratives in the coming years. I spoke with people who were in their late teens or early twenties in that phase. Mandal Commission, Ram Rath Yatra, Babri demolition, economic reforms, assassination attempt on a former prime minister, etc., were all big events in hindsight. And, all of them happened in the same phase. For the old, this was bit of a shock, but for the young, it was a defining phase. The youth did not have the baggage of history and were willing to reconsider a new narrative and fall on the right side of history. Those who did not fall on the side of the prevalant narrative waited and bided their time, built their arguments, found reasonings, and perhaps solutions. In many ways, they were also looking for the right amount of confidence to come out.

By 2010, many people who had been observing the developments of the 1990s and 2000s started coming of age. They began to develop better articulation and were seemingly more confident and less apologetic about their opinions and ideas. Taken together, the Hindutva movement and the economic reforms led to a more vibrant group of Indians who were economically better off and culturally more rooted. Yet, the number was far from the inflection point.

Well into the 2000s, the internet had begun to become an accessible commodity for many across the country. Social media platforms had propped up, which were being joined by people from across the world. It was a remarkable period wherein, for the first time, people were joining one another in cyberspace. Email had become the norm, and everyone's world was changing. But only a few understood the scale of the change about to happen.

As Orkut and Facebook brought communities together, people from within India began to talk to those who had shifted outside. Remember that the 1990s were about the brain drain in India. Some very smart people were shifting abroad because they perhaps could not get past the red tape (which characterized the functioning of the government back home), the socialist mindset, and fewer opportunities to grow. While many of these migrants made a comfortable living abroad, they did so in circumstances that were not conducive at all times. Also, the Indian diaspora, especially those who held on to their Indian passports, never had the occasion to forget that they came from a country that much of the West considered undeveloped; as a consequence, their passports were not held in high regard.

The reputation of an Indian passport has now increased tremendously under Prime Minister Modi's leadership. However, it is important to note here that as the internet and emails connected Indians spread across the world to their motherland, a certain reduction of space and distance happened. This shaped our early 2010s.

As the conversation over recent life updates began to get mundane, these platforms became hubs for conversations on nationalism, politics, culture, and so on. Right before was the age of Yahoo Messenger and other chat rooms on internet that helped people interact with each other in data. For many, this was life-changing. Indians in Tier 1 and Tier II cities began reaching out to the world, spreading their views and taking in those of the others.

Another trend that gained momentum was that of blogging. A little different from the modern-day vlogging—which documents an individual's life on video—blogging made the internet a digital diary to document thoughts, ideas, etc. In many ways, writing was revolutionized. As writers developed their ideas and began articulating, a larger number of them began writing on blogging websites and issuing long posts on social media platforms. These platforms also became avenues for those whose thoughts were perhaps too opinionated for the traditional media or the more 'mainstream' media. For the first time, the hold of opinion-makers who had ruled the roost for decades came under threat. Now, contrary opinions encompassing a great degree of nationalism and Indian-ness in terms of cultural ethos, as opposed to the socialist-communist and the so-called Left-liberal narrative, got into the mainstream.

Consider how reams of literature were written in the early 2000s about Hindu interests, the BJP, Narendra Modi, and the RSS. Talking favourably about Hindu interests in English academia had seemed parochial, even offensive, if not outright criminal. This can be traced to Macaulay's Minute and the influence of communism. Shockingly, these colonialists, with blood stains on their hands, ensured that the Hindu psyche had a blot on its forehead for generations to come as well.

Hence, it is important to recognize that what unfolded after 2014 has an independent, long history with compelling reasons. Around the mid-2000s, many young scholars and professionals who were doing well in their independent fields in India and across the world began noticing how their idea of Bharat was disconnected from the idea of India that was prevalent and propagated everywhere. During the course of the research, I also met those who had attended that famous rally when Sadhvi Ritambara exhorted out to a full house in Lutyens' Delhi, '*Kaho garv se, hum Hindu hain; Hindustan hamara hai.*'[2]

Another case in point is how our medieval times were written about as a sequence of battles that we, as native Indians, lost. Stories of Jat resistance against invaders or the glory of Vijayanagara, of the Ahoms, or of our maritime history were conveniently redacted. It left a generation so subdued subconsciously that it was tough to find a semblance of confidence. Perhaps, these tales were only preserved in our villages and oral history.

Noticing this, a few voices began to change the narrative. They stood on the tall legacy of Arun Shourie, Sita Ram Goel, and Ram Swarup, among others. They were mostly in their late thirties or forties, had an alternate and more confident version of their past shared over generations, had some common agonies, and found internet platforms as their medium. Blog posts and Facebook acted as the media to share those views. In no time, Indians all over the world, who could articulate their views, began connecting. This common belief strengthened the bonds and led to a global resurgence of Indic thoughts.

The Changing Scenario

A change began setting in around 2010, with strengthened voices and a 'freer' platform. This was also the time when Modi's graph as the chief minister of Gujarat was on a continual rise. While the NDA failed to convince the larger population in the 2009 general assembly elections, a change was brewing. Corruption, endangered internal security, scandals, and a dipping economy—all marked the declining status of India on the global stage, even as local issues made the state of the nation depressive for Indians. Against this backdrop, Modi emerged on the national stage. Having won another state election, he seized attention as a possible national leader.

Both of these developments coincidentally converged around 2013. Modi's election campaign, apart from other things, included speeches at select events across the country. A good part of the campaign was led by people who were intellectually and academically inclined towards the Indic thought process. History, economics, and cultural themes were discussed. Along with it, the idea of Bharat became an important topic.

In a sense, it was very similar to how the RSS shakhas teach swayamsevaks about the history of India. Hence, Modi's emergence had as equal an intellectual footing as any other weapon in his arsenal. One can argue that it was perhaps the most important one. Around this time, many people who would become popular in the coming years began writing what they thought about contemporary politics, Congress, dramas, scandals, the absolute treachery at the hands of a select few, the idea of India, etc. However, such narratives, although increasing in number, could not manage enough traction as the nation's politics was dominated by the Nehru–Gandhi family.

Perhaps for this reason, in some ways, the early contemporary revolution in writing began taking shape outside India, with little support from those in the country. Of course, there were those like Arun Shourie, who had made an impact over the decades as an independent voice, speaking for free markets, Hindutva, etc.

Similar is the case of Dr Bibek Debroy, who perhaps fitted into the same academic framework and intellectual integrity of stalwarts like Sitaram Goel and Ram Swarup. Dr Debroy's contribution to the nationalist narrative has been considerable. Apart from the books he wrote, which give an insight into the Hindu faith, he has published many translations of texts such as the Mahabharata and the Puranas. He is perhaps the first one to undertake this mammoth activity on a large scale. By doing so, he gave readers in English a dharmic understanding of our texts. This addition to the national narrative framework will surely help future generations who wish to understand the intellectual bandwidth in the Indic space. Prior to his works, the only English translations of Bharatiya and dharmic books were those done by colonizers or other Westerners, which, some may argue, had many words but little meaning.

Around the same time, economist Sanjeev Sanyal was mulling over many things Indian. While still working and living in Singapore, he published his first book, *The Indian Renaissance*. The book did well. To understand Sanyal's thought process, it is perhaps best to go back in time and soak in the interesting stories of the family bard (which would be a few elders) would share. The Sanyals come from a clan that is both rebellious and intellectual. Sanjeev's forefather, Sachindranath Sanyal, was a tall figure in the revolutionary struggle for Indian Independence, who also authored *Bandi Jeevan*. He was not alone, though; many others in the family accomplished great things over the years.

However, Sanjeev Sanyal is of a generation that was in college around the early 1990s, when India was going through a major economic and social upheaval: economic reforms, caste movements, the Ram Mandir campaign, the Rajiv Gandhi assassination, etc. All these events had an impact on his worldview. It took time before he developed his thoughts, added intellectual depth, and found the voice and a medium to project his views. Perhaps, this was the case with many others who had begun writing a new story about India by 2010. Sanjeev Sanyal, soon after the success of *The Indian Renaissance* and after having attained reasonable professional success, took a break. What unfolded over the next couple of years was his exploration of India, or Bharat.

Sanyal travelled around the country, documenting stories of this vast land, and built a popular non-fiction guide for many—and perhaps a direction for many others—in the form of another book titled *Land of the Seven Rivers*. This book, in many ways, opened the doors to unconventional thinking or an alternate view of history for many. He went around the country, delivering lectures on the book and building an alternate historical narrative of India. Interestingly, he was also organizing lectures in the run-up to the 2014 polls. He was nudging people towards the BJP's understanding of economics and, of course, Narendra Modi.

If one looks back, the impact of his book on Indian popular non-fiction writing (or rather history writing) has been remarkably important. I know many who have been inspired by him to promote our civilizational glory and Indian heritage, thereby being committed to the cause of a stronger nation. In fact, in some ways, it could very well be called the 'Sanyal school of thought'. For instance, tech entrepreneur Rahul Dewan started Sangam Talks after reading the book and interacting with Sanyal.

Hence, what Sanyal did essentially was not just write books. Instead, he was trying to create a framework of nationalist intellectualism. Before *Land of the Seven Rivers*, the thought process on some broad questions related to India, its heritage, its civilization, and on Ashoka, Akbar, Chhatrapati Maharaj, Islamic invasion and the resistance to it, etc., were little discussed and rather lopsided. Sanyal and his book offered a fresh look at Indian history. And this came not from an academic but an intellectual who was an expert on the economy. Perhaps, it was Sanyal's family legacy behind the writing.

I remember meeting Sanyal in 2015 after I had read the book. It was in Bengaluru for a writers' workshop where Sanyal spoke to many budding opinion-makers about the importance of Indic writing and, more importantly, why we should be telling our own stories. As the African proverb says, 'Until the lions have their own storyteller, the story of the hunt will always glorify the hunter.'

Several other writers have been taking the Indic project forward over the years. For example, Padma Shri Meenakshi Jain—a historian and political scientist and the author of *Ram and Ayodhya* and *The Battle for Rama: Case of the Temple at Ayodhya*—has kept the Indic flag flying high. Similarly, there is Vikram Sampath, who has authored bestsellers like the biography of Veer Savarkar and more. He also gave structure to many writing fellowships, literary festivals, and more, leading by example. Then there is J. Sai Deepak, the author-advocate whose *India That Is Bharat* and *India, Bharat and Pakistan* form part of the Bharat trilogy (the third is yet to be published), which offers a new perspective on the narrative of colonialism and compels the readers to look afresh at our history.

It would be pertinent here to add that India's civilizational and cultural depth was reflected also in present-day fictional writing in English. Two prominent authors whose books have not only been bestsellers but have also in full measure projected the country's cultural richness are Amish Tripathi and Ashwin Sanghi. While Amish has established himself for retelling our epics with a unique flavour and twist, Sanghi has written thrillers that hover around India's cultural symbols and iconography—they are appropriately categorized in the 'Bharat series'.

It was not just writers that emerged but also publishers who decided to promote the new narrative. Some of them had been around for a while, but they came into their own after 2014. Among the publishers who have made a mark in promoting India's cultural richness through the books they presented are BluOne Ink, Garuda, Aryan, Vitasta and Prabhat Prakashan, to name a few. In fact, even the bigger publishing houses that were earlier wary of accepting alternative narratives began to show greater enthusiasm with the changing times. For them writing was business and more readers would give them profits.

The new writers admittedly had a tough task dismantling the decades of distorted narratives that had been ensconced in the minds of the public. Indian authors had poisoned the thinking of readers with their jaundiced views. The Western media has, of course, been at the game for a long time but has been especially caustic in its treatment of the Modi era. The Western press has not shied away from twisting facts and figures to present a grim picture of India.

Not surprisingly, therefore, a good part of the readership abroad, not having visited India or had a first-hand experience of its social structure or its politics, has been influenced by the disrupted writing. Take, for example, the Western media's coverage of the situation arising in India from the COVID-19 pandemic. First, it was compared with the 1918 Spanish Flu! The media proceeded to slam the Government of India. This was in contrast to what many experts across the world had said—that India had handled the crisis remarkably well. Thereafter, questions were raised on the safety and efficacy of the vaccines that Indian agencies had developed in record time. The fact that these vaccines saved millions of lives not just in India but also abroad was conveniently downplayed.

A New Kind of Films

It was not just literature that was touched by the revival of interest in India's cultural and civilizational richness. A few film-makers took the daring step to tackle nationalist subjects and showed courage in depicting what had been taboo for decades because it went against the 'secular' sentiment of the powers-that-be and the elite fed on communism, Nehruvian ideals, and Macaulay's theories.

Vivek Agnihotri's *The Kashmir Files* was an unapologetic and blunt film that showed the trauma of Kashmir's persecuted

Hindus and the apathy of the political system. There were also films that celebrated the bravery of our armed forces and their successes against enemy nations. Among them, *Uri: The Surgical Strike* recorded remarkable success. The film is about India's retaliatory surgical strike inside Pakistan-occupied Kashmir against militants, following the terrorist attack on the Uri military base. More recently, came *Article 370*, which told the story of the abrogation of Article 370 and the politics that preceded and followed it.

Of course, critics of the Modi government were quick to dismiss these films as 'propaganda'. But the films told the stories as they ought to be told, and the audiences gave them a thumbs-up—yet another indication that mindsets had indeed changed, and for the better.

*

In 2014, Prime Minister Narendra Modi took office with much fanfare. Alongside, the intelligentsia inclined towards the BJP had begun to give shape to an alternate understanding of India. In fact, even before the polls, some people had begun getting together and mobilizing funding and resources. Some got together to start a digital magazine called *Swarajya*. In 2014, propelled by Modi's eventual ascension to prime ministership, a select few people began thinking of developing a platform that could become an umbrella organization for writing for thought-leaders and intellectuals. Do note that when somebody in India calls a section right-wing, they do not necessarily mean the economic right or the right as perhaps seen in the West. Instead, it could be the dharmic right or a mix of economy, civilization, and history, which is more in tune with our roots.

Creation and Revival of Forums

Originally, *Swarajya* was launched as a weekly magazine in 1956 by a journalist, Khasa Subba Rao, under the patronage of C. Rajagopalachari, who was a prominent freedom fighter and one of the founders of the Swatantra Party. The magazine promoted individual freedom as well as freedom of enterprise—it thus pitted itself against Nehru's socialist pattern. After Rajaji's death, the magazine's health declined, and it ceased publication subsequently.

The magazine was relaunched as an online daily in September 2014, with Sandipan Deb as the editorial director. The first edition of the revived print magazine was launched in January 2015.

Sometime later, came another portal *OpIndia*, which too promoted cultural nationalism and the 'right' point of view. Over time, it has gained for itself a committed readership. There were others preceding it like Faking News and more.

*

During house-shifting recently, I found my slam book from my early teen years. For those of you who may not know what a slam book is, it is (or was) a record-keeping notebook that teenagers would pass among each other and document their responses to the questions in it. For some reason, I had also kept one. I had perhaps recorded it when I was twelve. The slam books would have interesting questions for teenagers like: What do you want to become and more? One wonders if anyone really understood the depth of the question, leave aside knowing the answer. And, it occurs to me that it makes an interesting read—for knowing what we wanted to do and realizing what we are doing today.

The first entry in the slambook is usually of the owner of the diary. With ten stacks of books around me, which were brought down from the shelves for shifting, I sat cross-legged on the floor and thought of taking a quick look. While there were many entries from my friends from school that were amusing, my own became an eye-opener. Remember, I had absolutely forgotten about the notebook. I had no idea of its existence until then.

To the question of what motivated me, I had responded that I wanted to work for the well-being of my fellow Indians. In another, which asked what I wanted to become in the future, I had written that I wanted to be an IAS officer. Looking back, I think it was surprisingly yet fundamentally clear at an early stage in life that I wanted to commit myself to working for the people and our country. My inspiration was my grandfather. His honesty, hard work, and principled living had inspired thousands across Haryana. I was just hoping to continue working in the direction he laid out for us. With that same motivation, I had begun preparing for the civil services exam in 2012. Around the same time, Chief Minister Modi had begun making enough rumblings in Delhi.

In 2014, soon after *Swarajya* was launched, I made some progress in my preparations. As a student preparing for civil services, I was learning a lot more about our country, its civilization, history, politics, freedom fighters, etc. As I prepared myself for the subjective-type questions for the mains, I began writing on politics and history. And, it was during one of those breaks when I read about Swarajya in *The Hindu* newspaper and promptly sent a cold mail to *Swarajya.* As chance would have it, I was welcomed, and in no time I had begun writing for the magazine as well!

At this point, I think it is important to mention entrepreneur Hari Kiran Vadlamani, who established, supported financially, and envisioned a group of Indic intellectuals who could be connected to each other on a common platform. These people could be sitting in different cities all across the country and would eventually develop local chapters of people with a similar thought process. Much like *Swarajya*, the Indic Academy thus established by Vadlamani was supported by a similar set of people in Bengaluru or connected to Bengaluru.

While many plans were taking shape, the academy began organizing a book club called the Indic Book Club. Books on dharma, nationalist history, civilizational glory, and our collective past were shared among the members.

Around the same time, courtesy of the club and *Swarajya* magazine, I was invited to a writers' workshop in Bengaluru. As I look back, it is remarkable and even rewarding to see that so many people who were part of the group have been doing well in the intellectual space. Sanjeev Sanyal was one of the biggest attractions as he shared his work, motivated us, and gave insight into the steps ahead. It was there that, for the first time, I saw the potential of Indic writers and how they were perhaps going to shape the near future.

As I write this, I am finding it a little difficult to document the contributions of the many people who were brought there and what they built in the following years. Ashish Dhar took over as a dharmic intellectual and began the Indic Collective Trust, Pragyata, and later Upword. In fact, I remember discussing the importance of short-form content and how a well-constructed argument backed with facts and reasoning, packaged in impactful branding, could make a big difference in the prevalent intellectual discourse.

There was Pune-based Shefali Vaidya, who had become an Indic warrior on social media. Her clarity of thought and arguments have impressed hundreds of thousands of her followers. She also talked about Goa—the Hindu Goa that suffered at the hands of the Portuguese—which only a few know of. There were more, such as filmmaker Vivek Agnihotri; author, scientist, and analyst Anand Ranganathan; Rahul Roushan (the founder of *OpIndia*), and many others.

The academy also had an email group. Bengaluru South MP Tejasvi Surya was there. So was the national spokesperson of the BJP, Guru Prakash Paswan, and Bharatiya Janata Yuva Morcha's vice president, Abhinav Prakash. Email threads on wide-ranging topics that were more civilizational than political took shape.

At the same time, India Foundation also established itself as a premier think tank for further research on Indic topics. While the foundation organized many events, it was the Ideas Conclave that expanded this grouping of nationalist or right-wing intellectuals. In fact, it brought together many like-minded individuals and, in many ways, nudged them into writing. For instance, I got into a conversation with Makarand Paranjape, Sunil Ambekar, and Ashish Chauhan in the Delhi edition in 2017. Ideas Conclave was, in fact, a Ram Madhav (BJP General Secretary) show that organized yearly editions of the event. He brought together many people who were under the larger right-wing–dharmic–nationalist umbrella, giving the thought process a space to flourish and grow. Such efforts also inspired many others. Think tanks began taking shape. They would organize events, workshops, and lecture series on topical matters and motivate the younger generation to write essays and articles.

The internet again had a large impact on these developments. Around the same time, Mukesh Ambani-led Reliance Industries launched the Jio 5G network, which perhaps gave the fastest internet at the cheapest rates in the world. So far, nationalists who were finding it difficult to voice their opinions in the mainstream media were blogging and writing for digital platforms. After the launch of 5G, videos and podcasts became the preferred route for outreach. Even more, one's social media strength, that is, followers and subscription base, became a direct medium to interact with like-minded people.

It is well known that Twitter, Facebook, and YouTube were important mediums for Modi in his 2014 campaign. He opened a large door for many, many people to join his campaign. With cheaper internet, voices began filtering in from all parts of the country. Soon enough, historical wrongs began to trickle into regular conversations more often than ever.

It is only natural, then, that soon after Modi came to power, the *Swarajya* magazine took on a new shape. Around the same time, the Indic Book Club established its foundations. Similarly, other think tanks of nationalist orientation, such as the India Foundation, Vision India Foundation, and others, made their base. Already established think tanks like the Vivekananda International Foundation, among others, expanded their work. Many thinkers began writing more furiously. A crop of new and young writers began yielding results.

The credit for this momentum largely goes to the arrival of Narendra Modi on the national stage as the country's prime minister. With his own words and actions, he energized the revival of nationalist writing and nationalist film-making. But, I would argue that years on, there is much to be done.

7

Affordable and Humane Healthcare

Like many kids, I too, as a child, did not particularly look forward to visiting hospitals, especially a government hospital. I remember keeping clear of the hospital close to my alma mater, Hans Raj College, University of Delhi, during my graduation days. The medical waste all around, the long queues of glum-looking patients, and the worried looks of those accompanying them—the general apathy prevalent in government hospitals lent a tragic air to an institution that one visited to be cured and return healthy from.

I recall an incident in Panipat when I was driving back from a bus stand over a decade ago. It was early in the morning and the roads were reasonably empty. Nearing an otherwise secluded spot, I saw two people standing by the roadside. As I got nearer, I found a man lying on the road, bleeding from some fragments of a broken headlight of a motorcycle. I promptly got out of the car, requested them to help me pick the man up, and took him to the civil hospital. This man was hurt in the head and required immediate attention. I rushed through the fortunately minor, early morning traffic. Believing that, given the patient's condition, there would be instant medical attention available.

But nothing appeared to be in place. The stretcher, the compounder, the nurse, the doctor—I could find nobody. A life was at stake, and I was shouting desperately in the corridors for someone to hear my plea and guide me in a direction that would save the man's life. He had been bleeding as he lay on the back seat of my car. He was breathing heavily, seething with pain, and slowly losing comprehension.

A guard, smoking a beedi, was coaxed into action, and he grudgingly decided to help me out. It took one full hour before things began to fall into place. The doctor patched him and referred him to PGI, Rohtak. It took another forty-five minutes before an ambulance finally took off for Rohtak. I was, perhaps, in my first year of college, and it was during the UPA government. The apathy was visible and even more, it was normal. Nobody cared.

Cut to 2020. The world, clasped in the tentacles of the COVID-19 pandemic, was gasping for breath, literally and figuratively. The shadow of death and destruction loomed large all around, and India was no exception. People were dying. Hospital beds and ventilators were far too few, oxygen cylinders ran out of stock, and personal protection equipments (PPEs) were in inadequate numbers. And, of course, there was no vaccine, either in India or anywhere in the world, to counter the rampaging coronavirus. I felt the same sense of helplessness that I had experienced in Panipat civil hospital decades ago. Except that, this time around there was a prime minister who had come into office assuring that he would fix the status of the health sector in the country.

The Leader Leads

Modi's proactive measures, decisive actions, and steadfast commitment to safeguarding public health and economic well-being helped India navigate through those challenging times. As the nation fought the pandemic, with negativity in the air (and in the media) about the death count, Modi remained focused on the breakthroughs needed to repel the virus's attack. He took the lead, personally interacting with the stakeholders—from government agencies to the private sector—to find solutions. The commitment bore fruit. India developed one vaccine and manufactured another in record time, which saved millions of lives. It even exported the vaccines to needy countries. Oxygen-producing plants were set up at a rapid pace, and soon India was also producing enough PPEs to meet requirements. But for his firm leadership, there is no doubt that the impact of the catastrophe could have been far greater than it was on the country.

As humans evolved into civilizations, so did the complications that targeted them. It is from this perspective that this story should be seen. When a dangerous and life-threatening virus spreads across the world, there is only one way to tackle it: everyone must come together to face it. And defeat it.

That is what India did when Prime Minister Modi launched the Vaccine Maitri Mission. The pandemic was more than just a black swan event. It shocked the global system and countries, and economies were destroyed. Amidst these circumstances, what became clear was how more prosperous economies wanted to hoard vaccines and other medical supplies for themselves. This left the smaller nations to their own travails. Even as the pleas for support got louder, many countries held a begging bowl for medical support.

Standing tall as the leader of the Global South, the Government of India, under Modi's leadership, resolved to support these countries, even as it itself was battling the crisis. The COVID-19 vaccines were exported all across the world, winning the hearts of people. At a high-level United Nations General Assembly meeting in September 2021, many world leaders openly thanked India for this support.

Recognizing the gravity of the situation, Modi swiftly initiated proactive measures to combat the spread of the virus within the country. The first of these was a complete nationwide lockdown. Everything, except the most essential services, was shut down. Transportation services ground to a halt, and people remained where they were. Offices were closed, and commercial activities ceased to function. Of course, the decision led to tremendous problems, with the poor being the hardest hit. But in those early months, a lockdown was the only measure available to contain the spread of the virus; the lockdown helped save tens of thousands of precious lives.

Alongside this, the government swiftly scaled up healthcare infrastructure across the country. Temporary hospitals were set up, COVID-19 testing facilities were expanded, and efforts were made to ramp up the production of essential medical supplies, such as PPE kits and ventilators. The government also launched the PM CARES Fund to support healthcare infrastructure and relief measures, demonstrating a commitment to bolstering the nation's healthcare response.

Also, understanding the economic repercussions of the lockdown, especially on the poor and smaller businesses, the government rolled out a series of economic stimulus packages and relief to the vulnerable sections of society.

Direct cash transfers, free food grains, and welfare schemes were implemented to mitigate the impact of the pandemic-induced economic downturn on the poor and marginalized communities.

Made in India Vaccines

Under PM Modi's watch, India launched one of the world's largest vaccination drives, aiming to inoculate millions of Indians against the virus. Through efficient planning and execution, India achieved remarkable milestones in vaccination coverage, showcasing the prime minister's commitment to safeguarding public health and achieving herd immunity. More than 220 crore COVID-19 vaccine doses were administered as of 6 January 2023; 97 per cent of the eligible beneficiaries had received at least one dose, while 90 per cent had received both doses. The COWIN platform, a web initiative, provided real-time stock tracking at the national, state, and district levels and helped plug wastage of vaccines.

I was working with Rath Foundation (which was organizing donations and medical support in Haryana, Chandigarh, Delhi, etc.) and was a witness to the transformations in the medical industry that, in many ways, Modi has ushered in.

Made in India vaccines were also the focal point of all media, even the Western media. While Pfizer, like other pharmaceutical companies, sought authorization for its vaccine in India, Modi remained steadfast in his commitment to evaluating the safety and efficacy of vaccines to protect the Indian population. Modi's government engaged in negotiations with Pfizer on terms that were favourable to India's interests. This included discussions on pricing, procurement agreements, liability clauses, and technology transfer for vaccine production. Modi's determination against the aggressive drive by foreign vaccine makers fetched him many critics; even in India, sections of the media, perhaps incentivized, raised questions. But Modi remained unfazed. India's interests came first, he said bluntly.

Prime Minister Modi bolstered efforts to ramp up domestic vaccine production capacity. Initiatives such as the collaboration with indigenous vaccine manufacturers, Bharat Biotech and the Serum Institute of India, played a crucial role in enhancing India's vaccine manufacturing capabilities. The government ensured that clearances for the manufacturing of vaccines came swiftly by cutting through red tape, without compromising on the established safety protocols. Government institutions, such as the Indian Council of Medical Research and the National Institute of Virology, worked in tandem with the vaccine manufacturers to meet the urgent needs of the country.

When a country's leader is seen right in the front ranks during a crisis, people as a composite mass rise to the occasion, driven by a national resolve and the motto: 'We shall not give up; we shall overcome.' India's successful handling of the COVID-19 calamity—better than some of the developed nations that had superior healthcare infrastructure and other resources—drew praise from across the world.

In April 2022, as India was slowly recovering from the pandemic, I remembered how the crisis posed unimaginable challenges for the healthcare system in India. Over the last two years, organizations, systems, and governance saw, in some sense, a reboot. It was, however, in no way an easy ride. However, one could convincingly argue two things: First, had it not been for Modi's leadership, India would have seen much worse. And second, compared to the world and keeping in mind its population, India did much better than many.

In the same month, the *New York Times* published an article written by editor and author Jyoti Thottam, which opened with the words:

> In the spring of 1947, nothing about the future of India, its identity as a nation or the kind of country it would be, was certain. India would soon be free from British colonial rule, but it could not fulfil the basic needs—let alone the hopes and ambitions—of most of its people. That would require new institutions, new ideas, and men and women who were willing to take a chance on building them.[1]

The piece was mostly adapted from a book that the author had written, giving insights into how healthcare was after Independence. But it led me to an enquiry of my own. Both Prime Minister Narendra Modi and Nobel laureate economist Amartya Sen agree on how education and health are two important determinants of social and economic progress. Yet, after seventy-five years, how does healthcare fare in the country, and where does it stand?

The question has perhaps been raised by many. In fact, I vividly remember discussing these challenges when I was preparing for the civil services examination. This was also a time when the Gujarat model of governance had made enough waves in the country. Around the same time, Delhi, where I was based, was feeling the tremors of a massive anti-corruption movement, and the Nehru–Gandhi electoral dominance was being rightly questioned in different quarters.

History of Healthcare in India

Modi has brought about a monumental change in the priorities and functioning of the government concerning healthcare. However, before we go there, it is important to know how medicine and health were seen in India in the past. Western medicine in India is an indirect product of British colonial ambitions in the country. Surgeons were brought in when the colonialists came, and, over time, the medical service came into being. Notably, it began with the military and became a part of the civil service only later. As a result, at the time of Independence, India's medical infrastructure was in a dismal state.

The Health Survey and Development Committee, popularly known as the Bhore Committee, remains incredibly significant even eighty years later. The committee was set up to study the existing position of health conditions and health organizations in India and to make recommendations for future development. Amidst the turmoil of the Second World War and the Quit India Movement, the British government in India announced the creation of the panel on 18 October 1943, with Sir Joseph William Bhore as its chairman. Bhore recruited over two dozen British and Indian doctors, along with colonial public health officials, to serve on his committee and despatched them all across India.

Bhore was born in Nashik and educated in Pune and London. He joined the Indian Civil Service in 1902. He was assigned to the Madras cadre and had a long and glorious career in the civil service before retiring with a knighthood in 1935. During this time, he served as the dewan of Cochin state, worked as acting high commissioner for India in the UK, served as secretary to the Government of India, and even became a member of the governor general's executive council.[2]

The committee's report was an eye-opener. It brought to life the failures of the colonial regime. Apart from that, it also provided solutions to fix the problems. The committee's report began with a comparison of India's health situation with other countries and its poor status in important metrics.

Table 1. Comparison of Mortality and Life Expectancy

					1987			
	Death Rate	IMR	Life Expectancy at Birth		Death	Life Expectancy		
Country	(1937)	(1937)	Males	Females	Death Rate	IMR	Male	Female
New Zealand	9.1	31	65.04	67.88 (1931)	9	11	72	78
Australia	9.4	38	63.48	67.14 (1932-34)	8	10	73	80
Union of S. Africa	10.1	37	57.78	61.48 (1925-27) (Europeans only)	10	72	58	64
					(Blacks & White)			
Canada	10.2	76	59.32	61.59 (1929-31)	8	8	73	80
U.S.A.	11.2	54	59.12	62.67 (Whites)	9	10	72	74
			47.55	49.51 (Blacks)	(Blacks & White)			
Germany	11.7	64	59.86	62.75 (1932-43)	12	8	72	78
					(W. Germany)			
England & Wales	12.4	58	58.74	62.88 (1930-32)	12	9	72	78
Italy	14.2	109	53.76	56.00 (1930-32)	10	10	74	80
France	15.0	65	54.30	59.02 (1928-33)	10	8	74	80
Japan	17.0	106	44.82	46.54 (1926-30)	7	6	75	81
Java	18.8	–	–	–	9	71	58	62
					(Indonesia)			
Palestine	18.9	153	–	–	–	–	–	–
Ceylon	21.7	158	–	–	6	33	68	73
British India	22.4	162	26.91	26.56 (1921-30)	11	99	58	58
Egypt	27.2	165	–	–	10	85	59	62

The committee noted that the health conditions of children and women were distressingly bleak. It revealed that a staggering 48 per cent of all deaths in India were among children under the age of ten—a sharp contrast to the mere 10 per cent recorded in England and Wales. Additionally, maternal mortality was at an alarming rate of twenty per 1,000 childbirths in India; it stood at a significantly lower level of around three per 1,000 in England.

The main causes behind this bleak condition were (i) unsanitary conditions, (ii) impaired nutrition, and (iii) insufficiency of existing medical and preventive health infrastructure. In addition, there was a general lack of medical education, which must be seen in consonance with the general apathy towards affairs in India. Alongside poverty, there was mass unemployment in India. As former Prime Minister Manmohan Singh put it, the brightest jewel in the British Crown was the poorest country in the world in terms of per capita income at the beginning of the twentieth century.[3]

However, the committee added,

> It is not for us to apportion responsibility for the sombre realities which face us today. It is with the future that we are concerned and if the picture is to be substantially altered for the better with the least possible delay, a nation-wide interest must be aroused and the irresistible forces of an awakened public opinion essayed in the war against disease.

The committee was clear that the healthcare problem in India had a very composite character, and solving only one dimension would not address the issue. In fact, such an approach would be a waste of both time and effort. Further, the committee recommended a slew of measures towards a national health plan.

The committee also recommended whole-time salaried service, focusing on both the preventive and curative aspects of medicine, and garnering support from medical and auxiliary professions, including dentists, pharmacists, and nurses, to augment the service. Healthcare, then, would be integrated—curative, preventive, and promotive for the entire population. Further, the report also laid out the financial allocation for medical relief and public health. While the details are interesting for a book on public health, it would be fair to highlight here that from financial allocations to the plan proposed, most parts of the report were not implemented by the government in independent India.

In fact, it can be said that the committee, which the British must have hoped would give a good impression of their rule in India, showed a rather grim and gloomy reality. The report also laid out a solid plan for implementation in India that could transform the healthcare infrastructure in the country. An ideal that a soon-to-be independent nation would have thrived for. Says K. Sujatha Rao in her book *Do We Care*, 'The exhaustive Joseph Bhore report of 1946 was a classic then and continues to be one even now.'[4]

Healthcare after 1947

When India achieved independence in 1947, it found itself in a precarious situation. Centuries of being an economic resource for Britain had left the country impoverished, with the riches it once possessed traded for illiteracy, poverty, and widespread hunger and malnutrition. Overall life expectancy was a mere thirty-two years. It had slightly improved from about twenty-six years of age (as mentioned in the Bhore Committee report). Shockingly, the infant mortality rate was as high as 145.6 per 1,000 live births, and the maternal mortality ratio in the 1940s was a staggering 2,000 per 100,000 live births.

To compound these challenges, a mere 50,000 doctors were serving the entire country, and only 725 primary healthcare centres were struggling to cover an immense area of over 3,287,263 square kilometres. Hence, the immediate task facing independent India's first set of leaders was nothing short of herculean. Over the years, to address these challenges, some steps were taken, like the vaccination programmes and the setting up of the All India Institute of Medical Science (AIIMS). However, most of it was small compared to the magnitude of the problem.

Immediately after India became a republic, the economy followed a planning model. The model, in many ways, ensured that India's progress in the health sector was rather stunted. Another reason was the fact that health was a state subject. However, the overall economy was not showing considerable progress and Congressian politics, which, many would argue, worked on a 'development deficit', failed to make meaningful advances. States were notably in a financial crunch and had to prioritize many things apart from healthcare. As a consequence, states were always dependent on the Centre for funds. This opened doors for foreign grant aid organizations to make an entry into the Indian healthcare system.

K. Sujatha Rao writes,

> Thus, during these first three decades of India's planned development, the health system was being shaped by three broad approaches. First, there was the dominant policy focus on controlling infectious diseases and family planning. The programmatic needs of these priorities then influence the organization of primary health. Second, the focus was on teaching hospitals to produce the required human resources. Third, due to limited resources and weak prioritization, investments required for building a sound foundation of primary care were patchy and grossly inadequate.

Notably, the benefits of tilting towards the urban areas were vivid too. Indigenous medicine was also seemingly ignored. Budgetary allocations leaned heavily towards Western medical practices. Those who were trained in Ayurveda and homeopathy were left with crumbs to work with.

Commentators today would argue that the entire system was pervasively serving only the affluent.

Such was the state of affairs that healthcare limitations were treated as normal by the people, barring a privileged few who had access to the best in the country and abroad. While it's difficult to find written references, Hindi films did show the right-sized mirror. There have been films on the big screen from the 1960s to the 1980s that show deaths due to tuberculosis, poor drugs supply, an extreme shortage of blood in the hospital, and lack of ambulances to take patients to hospitals, among others. To top it all, there was the cost of healthcare.

Take, for instance, the 1977 film *Anurodh*, wherein the protagonist sings in a show to earn enough to save his friend's life. Or *Kala Patthar*, which depicts the medical facilities or absence thereof in the lives of miners.

The issue of red tape and favouritism that corrupted the healthcare sector was tackled too. Take the example of *Ek Doctor ki Maut*. Dr Dipankar Roy (played brilliantly by Pankaj Kapur) discovers a vaccine for leprosy. He finds recognition all over the country and abroad, but his seniors are miffed. He is consistently harassed and humiliated, and his breakthrough is downplayed and demeaned, leaving him shattered.

While films may have used creative freedom to send the message, who could argue that the situation on the ground was any different?

Modi's Tryst with Healthcare

In line with the global goal Alma-Ata declaration of 'Health for All', the Government of India brought the first National Health Policy over three decades after India became independent. That the idea of primary healthcare found its roots during these times is an important development of this phase.

It is on these principles and logic that Prime Minister Modi would focus his efforts decades later.

After the National Health Policy 1982, corporate healthcare also began taking root in India. With the economic reforms of the 1990s, this expanded, and yet good healthcare stayed expensive, if not out of reach for a large section of Indians. As India marched into the twenty-first century, the healthcare disparities were glaringly evident. Private healthcare was a booming business, and the government appeared to have abandoned its responsibility.

The 1990s saw a long phase of coalition politics in India. No national political party was able to garner enough votes to win a simple majority in Parliament. Several sectors, including healthcare as a policy matter subject, were relegated to the background as parties continued to jostle for space and power.

The situation changed drastically when Modi came to power. The importance he gave to health and cleanliness as chief minister of Gujarat would later guide his policies as prime minister too.

The 1979 tragedy in Morbi, Gujarat, caused the deaths of thousands of people when flash floods crashed through the Machchhu II dam. Modi, who was then an RSS worker, was not in the region when the tragedy happened; he learnt the details from the headquarters of a magazine in Mumbai. Within a day, he reached Morbi via Delhi and Rajkot. Modi, who was then Prant Vyavastha Pramukh, directed swayamsevaks to find dead bodies and connect the lost ones with their families. He, with support from senior leaders, arranged for a rehabilitation programme. Reportedly, during the relief work, the visuals of him carrying sacks of grains on his back were also featured in the magazine.

Modi witnessed the challenges of sanitation and cleanliness. Knowing that stagnant water could give rise to disease, the problem was immediately tackled. It was also equally important to take care of food needs and effective civic management for people who had been displaced due to the floods. Medicines, sanitation facilities, and make-shift camps were all arranged without undue delay. The experience turned out to be useful when Modi became chief minister after the Bhuj earthquake of 2001. Even more, during the Kedarnath disaster, he ensured a systematic campaign that took utmost care of cleanliness, sanitation, medicine, and other special facilities for women and children. Hence, managing public health and the importance, thereof, was well engrained into him even before he took the office of the Prime Minister of India.

Healthcare in BJP's Manifesto

It was no surprise then that the BJP's manifesto after Modi was declared the party's prime ministerial face read:

> India needs a holistic care system that is universally accessible, affordable and effective and drastically reduces the out-of-pocket spending on health. NRHM has failed to meet the objectives and will be radically reformed. BJP accords high priority to health sector, which is crucial for securing the economy. The overarching goal of healthcare would be to provide, 'Health Assurance to all Indians and to reduce the out of pocket spending on health care', with the help of state governments.
>
> The current situation calls for radical reforms in the healthcare system with regard to national healthcare programmes and delivery, medical education and training, and financing of healthcare. Our government would focus on the following reforms in healthcare:[5]

BJP manifesto for 2014 elections	Review remarks-2023
• the last healthcare policy dates back to 2002. India now needs a comprehensive healthcare policy to address the complex healthcare challenges, keeping in view the developments in the healthcare sector and the changing demographics. BJP will initiate the New Health Policy.	NHP-2017
• initiate the 'National Health Assurance Mission', with a clear mandate to provide universal healthcare that is not only accessible and affordable, but also effective, and reduces the OOP spending for the common man.	PM-JAY
• Education and Training - Will review the role of various professional regulatory bodies in healthcare and consider setting up an overarching lean body for healthcare. High priority will be given to address the shortfall of healthcare professionals.	Established NMC
• Modernize Government hospitals, upgrading infrastructure and latest technologies.	Multiple measures.
• Reorganize Ministry of Health and Family Welfare in order to converge various departments dealing in healthcare, food and nutrition and pharmaceuticals, for effective delivery of healthcare services.	Steps taken.
• Increase the number of medical and para-medical colleges to make India self sufficient in human resources, and set up an AIIMS like institute in every state.	(ADD DATA)
• Yoga and Ayurveda are the gifts of ancient Indian civilization to humanity and we will increase the public investment to promote Yoga and AYUSH. We will start integrated courses for Indian System of Medicine (ISM) and modern science and Ayurgenomics. We will set up institutions and launch a vigorous program to standardize and validate the Ayurvedic medicine.	National Ayush Mission etc.

BJP manifesto for 2014 elections	Review remarks-2023
• Move to pre-emptive care model where the focus and thrust will be on child health and prevention.	Mission Indradhanush-Intensified Mission Indradhanush-POSHAN Abhiyaan
• School health program would be a major focus area, and health and hygiene will be made a part of the school curriculum.	Swachh Bharat Abhiyan
• Focus on Rural Health care delivery.	Ayushman Bharat-PMJAY
• Senior Citizens healthcare would be a special focus area.	PMJAY
• Give high priority to chronic diseases, and will invest in research and development of solutions for chronic diseases like obesity, diabetes, cancer, CVD etc.	Ongoing
• Occupational health programs will be pursued aggressively.	Ongoing
• Utilize the ubiquitous platform of mobile phones for healthcare delivery and set up the 'National eHealth Authority' to leverage telemedicine and mobile healthcare for expanding reach and coverage and to define the standards and legal framework for technology driven care.	In progress
• Universalization of emergency medical services-108.	Done
• Re-orientation of herbal plants board to encourage farming of herbal plants.	Promoted

BJP manifesto for 2014 elections	Review remarks-2023
• Population stabilization would be a major thrust area and would be pursued as a mission mode program.	
• Programme for Women Healthcare with emphasis on rural, SC, ST and OBC in a mission mode.	Promoted
• Mission mode project to eradicate malnutrition.	Poshan Abhiyaan
• Launch National Mosquito Control mission.	
• Poor Hygiene and Sanitation have a far reaching, cascading impact. We will ensure a 'Swachh Bharat' by Gandhiji's 150th birth anniversary in 2019, taking it up in mission mode by converging resources and building around jan bhagidari:	Swachh Bharat Mission
• Create an open defecation free India by awareness campaign and enabling people to build toilets in their home as well as in schools and public places.	Swachh Bharat Mission
• Set up modern, scientific sewage and waste management systems.	Swachh Bharat Mission
• We will introduce Sanitation Ratings measuring and ranking our cities and towns on 'sanitation'; and rewarding the best performers.	Dashboard and e-Governance measures in different schemes included Swachh Bharat Mission
• Make potable drinking water available to all thus reducing water-borne diseases, which will automatically translate into Diarrhoea-free India."	Jal Jeevan Mission

Within the first few months as prime minister, Modi made his reflections on healthcare clear to the nation. While his interventions are discussed in detail in the following pages, it is important to get a sense of some other aspects of healthcare that his policies had a bearing on. He made it clear that prevention was one of the most important aspects of healthcare in India.[6] To that end, simply upgrading health facilities in the country was not good enough. Instead, a holistic approach to healthcare had to be adopted.

Apart from that, missions like Make In India and Digital India were also utilized for the larger cause of healthcare delivery in the country. His concern can also be gauged from the fact that over the years, any sector that impacted the health and well-being of Indians saw the prime minister putting in an extra effort to see it through.

PM Modi had begun going into the finer aspects and different blocs of health metrics as well. For instance, in October 2014, only a few months into power, he was sharing anguish at the state of maternal and neonatal care and primary healthcare in India.[7] Harsh Vardhan, a trained doctor, was appointed the first health minister of the Modi-led government. Notably, apart from his long experience in medicine, Dr Vardhan had experience in the polio pilot project. However, some months later, Jagat Prakash Nadda replaced Dr Vardhan as the minister of health and family welfare.

Both these leaders hold high positions in the party, and giving them the portfolio of health marked a departure from the tradition wherein the portfolio was not given to politically powerful or influential people. As Rao mentions in her book,

> Health is not a much sought after ministry as it has measly resources, poor policy, attention and low priority in the

eyes of the Prime Minister. This became evident when the coalition compulsions of the NDA and UPA1 lead to bartering the health ministry in lieu of political support from Pattali Makkal Katchi (PMK), a small party of Tamil Nadu that had about six MPs.[8]

Flagship Initiatives

Fresh into government, Prime Minister Modi began actively working towards the electoral agenda. A big shift was happening in governance at the Centre. An article from June 2014 in *The Economic Times* noted,

> As part of the drive to lift the pall of policy paralysis that dogged the Manmohan Singh government, the PM's decision to let ministers concerned take a call on the issues pending before the ministerial groups, some of which have been hanging fire for years, is an extension of the message he conveyed to them at his second cabinet meeting on Thursday. Apart from drawing up action plans for their first 100 days in office soon, ministers were asked to treat the resolution of 'all issues pending in their department, because of the old government or any other reason' as their number one agenda item.[9]

It is interesting to know that in the UPA's first term, there were over 125 ministerial groups for 'prickly' policy decisions, most of which were steered by senior minister Pranab Mukherjee. About ninety-five were formed in UPA-II. Thirty-three were still functioning when the UPA was shown the door in 2014—which loosely translates into failure in achieving their mandate.[10]

This was in stark contrast to what was expected and achieved in the coming years. Prime Minister Modi began personally intervening in and motivating different ministries of his government to achieve the objectives of flagship programmes. From inception to execution, his inputs have steered the course of any programs or work that a ministry does.

A proactive approach has become the hallmark of Modi's governance. For instance, when a fire broke out in a temple at Kollam, Kerala, due to some unauthorized fireworks in 2016, he quickly tasked Health Minister Nadda to reach the site at the soonest. Even more, he ensured that the minister reached the temple site and the hospital in the shortest time by mobilizing resources for swift travel. Modi too later visited the site and the hospital and extended all help to the state government and the injured.

Another incident pertains to a fire inside a hospital in Odisha due to lax measures. Nadda was on the ground and ensured that quick action was taken against the culprits.

Apart from proactive monitoring, Prime Minister Modi has a clear idea of the challenges that plague the Indian healthcare system. As chief minister, he had seen those challenges from close quarters and addressed them by focusing on preventive healthcare. To bridge the gaps in healthcare in the state, he also pushed for a stronger public-private partnership. It is this experience of keenly observing the challenges and gaps, identifying the root cause, discussing with stakeholders, finding a workable solution, implementing the programmes, seeking regular feedback, and ensuring consistency that he learnt during his chief ministership that came in handy once he became the prime minister.

In fact, he later recalled how, in his days as chief minister, he launched schemes like Swasthya Gujarat, Ujjwal Gujarat, and Mukhyamanti Amritam Yojna, which helped shape national-level policies and serve the poor. In order to improve the health and nutrition parameters of women and children,

Modi introduced Chiranjivi Yojna for institutional delivery, which benefitted over 14 lakh mothers in the state. The Chiranjivi and Khikhilahat Schemes were expanded at the national level into Mission Indradhanush and PM Matru Vandana Yojana.[11]

In a speech a few months into office as the prime minister, he also expressed concern over India's health indicators such as infant mortality and maternal mortality. PM Modi stated, 'Even if one child fell in a borewell, the entire country was worried, but we need to generate more awareness about the hundreds of children who are unable to survive due to lack of primary healthcare facilities.' He added, 'Society and Government should together give priority to the poorest of poor and make whatever efforts we can to provide affordable health services.'[12]

'Na gandagi karenge, na karne denge'

Swachh Bharat Abhiyaan has had a remarkable impact on public health in India. On the morning of 2 October 2014, Modi initiated the Clean India Mission from Rajghat, transforming it into a public movement that saw widespread participation. As the first head of government to launch an initiative that came with such formidable challenges, Prime Minister Modi's vision for the campaign extended from celebrities to the common person, from politicians to labourers, from governmental bodies to corporate entities—all playing a pivotal role in its success.

The launch of this campaign was more than just a governmental effort; it was a culmination of historical significance and cultural ethos. Modi artfully drew upon the indelible connection between hygiene and the Hindu way of life, as evident from the faith's revered teachings and long-standing customs. Moreover, he conscientiously highlighted the unfulfilled aspiration of Mahatma Gandhi and reminded the nation of Gandhi's visionary dream of an India that is not only free but also clean.

Prior to PM Modi's intervention, discussions on cleanliness often remained confined to the realms of meetings, seminars, and ornate events. The crucial element, the bottom-up approach, was strangely absent. Modi ingeniously blended these pieces. He amalgamated Gandhi's impactful slogan—transforming Quit India to Clean India—and emphasized that while India had gained independence, it was yet to achieve the state of cleanliness Gandhi had envisioned. Central to Modi's strategy was to inculcate a sense of ownership among the people. This was exemplified by his innovative method of crowd-sourcing symbol suggestions, in a way ensuring that the programme truly became a collective endeavour. Even social media was leveraged to spread the idea of the Swachh Bharat Mission widely.

In 2024, the movement has led to visible changes, not just around us but in health outcomes as well. Take, for example, the case of Panipat, an industrial town about 100 km north of Delhi, in the state of Haryana. The city is mentioned in our history books for epoch-defining battles. But its post-Independence history is replete with examples of business and entrepreneurial success. Early spinning mills were followed by more advanced technologies, and with time, the textile industry in the city boomed. As business flourished, more people converged into the town, first from the neighbouring villages and then from other districts. This was followed by the arrival of people from outside the state. In no time, the city's industrial area was full of labour quarters. Illegal colonies mushroomed in the peripheral sectors of the city to accommodate the growing workforce population.

In this quick advance, the city's public infrastructure was overwhelmed. A few years into the twenty-first century, the problem worsened. Open defecation in farm fields, near railway tracks, or at clogged drains was common. Much like how it happened in the villages across India, women would step out of their homes before the sun rose for their daily ablutions. The risks associated with it were treated like they were a regular part of life. Unsanitary conditions prevailed near Asandh Road, Bishan Saroop Colony, Noorwala, and Insar Bazar. Only a very few places in the city could be called clean and liveable. The situation in the villages was as bad, or worse.

This had to change. But how? The task was mammoth and required a mindset shift. It needed people to step out of their easy and sometimes selfish ways and to think for society. Emphasizing the importance of individual efforts, Prime Minister Modi said,

> Is the job of getting rid of filth belong to the *Safai karmchari* only? Isn't it the duty of all the 125 crore countrymen? Will we keep on imposing everything on them only? Something good happens or bad, will [we] keep on blaming them only? We have to change this situation. Like all 125 crore Indians the Prime Minister is also first son of Bharat Mata and Prime Minister later. Therefore, as the children of this mother, all of us are responsible that we should not keep our country like this. It may be the village neighbourhood, home family, school and college, mandir, masjid or gurdwara; how can we keep it dirty? Wherever we see filth or see someone throwing papers why don't we feel like picking that up? I know this will not be accomplished only by publicity campaign. Old habits take time to change. It's a difficult task, I know. But we have till 2019 when we will observe 150th anniversary of Mahatma Gandhi.

Swachh Bharat Mission was envisioned as a major, individual—and logically thereafter, community-driven—step towards improving the preventive healthcare system of the country. It aimed to provide universal sanitation coverage, improve cleanliness, and eliminate open defecation. The construction of individual household toilets, community and public toilets, and waste management were some key objectives to achieve. The Swachh Bharat Mission (Urban) and the Swachh Bharat Mission (Gramin) were the two components of the campaign. The Swachh Bharat Mission (Urban) is overseen by the Ministry of Urban Development, and the Swachh Bharat Mission (Gramin) by the Ministry of Drinking Water and Sanitation; the mission in its entirety is coordinated by the latter.

To implement it, the union and state governments utilized resources from multiple quarters. To streamline the implementation of the programme and its execution, a dashboard was established, which began documenting developments related to the programme on an almost real-time basis. From 2014 to 2019, 99.2 per cent of rural India was covered under this mission. Over 9.5 crore toilets have been constructed nationwide since October 2014, and 564,658 villages have been declared open-defecation-free. As of 14 June 2019, thirty states/union territories were completely covered with individual household latrines. Health outcomes have, predictably, greatly improved as a consequence of the mission.

Ten years later and after the changes that have taken place in that period, it is not easy to imagine where we are coming from. The presence of dustbins along roadsides, the hiring of private contractors for effective waste management by government or municipal authorities, cleaner railway stations and bus stands, and the proper disposal of medical waste outside hospitals are all outcomes of the Clean India Mission. One cannot argue that everything is shiny, clean, and beautiful and that as a country, we have achieved utopia, but considering where we were about a decade ago, the change is vivid, awe-inspiring, and uplifting. The following observation by a Panipat-based poultry feed manufacturer, Unnat, reflects this sentiment:

> I have been travelling to Uttar Pradesh and further since the mid-1990s for work. We have plants all over now. I would prefer sitting on a night train and arriving early morning to my destination for work. The stations were filthy. The toilets would be the worst dens of diseases. Some would even openly defecate in a corner of the platform. There was no cleaning staff and nobody seemed to care. I still prefer to go on some routes via train. The difference is starkly visible. I can now open my tiffin box and have it on the platform. This was unimaginable about a decade ago.

Squatting in open fields has visibly reduced over the years. In February 2021, the government introduced Swachh Bharat 2.0, with a primary focus on comprehensive faecal sludge management.

SBM's Dramatic Impact

Swachh Bharat Mission has had a clear impact on public health in India. With cleaner spaces, the potency and propensity of certain diseases have declined. Studies show that stillbirths have decreased. The number of low birth weight babies (newborns weighing less than 2.5 kg) and diarrhoea and malaria in children under the age of five too has come down—from around 6,968 cases in 2015 to 5,683 cases in 2019.

A study by the World Health Organization, 'Swachh Bharat Mission: Preliminary Estimations of Potential Health Impacts from Increased Sanitation Coverage', revealed that in 2014, prior to the launch of Swachh Bharat Mission, 140,000 deaths from diarrheal disease due to poor sanitation were reported, which significantly decreased to 50,000 in 2018, four years after the launch of the mission. Another study, this time by UNICEF conducted on behalf of the Ministry of Drinking Water and Sanitation, evaluated the financial benefits of SBM and found that every household in an open-defecation-free village saved around ₹50,000 per year by reducing the risk of diseases from just using toilets and proper sanitation.

Since the report also suggested that clean drinking water had helped reduce diseases, it is important to highlight another programme, the Jal Jeevan Mission, which envisions drinking water supply to every rural household. It was launched by Prime Minister Modi from the ramparts of the Red Fort on 15 August 2019, as India celebrated its seventy-third Independence Day. In September 2023, four years after the launch of the mission, the number of rural tap connections reached 13 crores (from just over three crores in 2019). This was a remarkable feat and a water revolution in every sense!

Ayushman Bharat Scheme

Arguably the biggest intervention in healthcare by the Modi government is the Ayushman Bharat Scheme. It is important to understand here that health is not a union subject. There are, therefore, conflicts in terms of the functionality of health schemes that are central in nature. Since the union government in earlier decades failed to deliver as per needs, state governments made their own fresh plans and strategies.

It was against this backdrop that the Modi government brought forth the Ayushman Bharat Scheme, also sometimes referred to as 'ModiCare'. It can be further understood from an ancient wisdom passed on since generations:

> Oṃ sarve bhavantu sukhinaḥ
> sarve santu nirāmayāḥ
> sarve bhadrāṇi paśyantu mā kaściddu ḥ khabhāgbhavetaı
> oṃ śāntiḥ śāntiḥ śāntiḥıı (verse 51, *Garuda Purana*)

The essence of the above lines from the final chapter of *Garuda Purana* resonates deeply with the cultural and spiritual ethos of India. This sentiment, advocating the welfare of all and the alleviation of suffering, finds a meaningful parallel in India's modern healthcare endeavours, including in Ayushman Bharat.

In 2017, based on the recommendations of the Task Force for Comprehensive Healthcare, the National Health Policy was launched. The National Health Policy 2017 emerged fourteen years after the previous one served as a declaration of purpose to initiate the journey towards universal health coverage. (The World Health Organization defines universal health coverage as ensuring that all individuals and communities have access to promotive, preventive, curative, rehabilitative, and palliative healthcare services of sufficient quality to be effective. This should be achieved without causing financial hardship, and it should promote equity in access, quality, and financial risk protection.) Additionally, in the same year, the new National Health Policy was adopted, which made it clear that around two-thirds of health funding would be directed at primary healthcare. To that end, Ayushmann Bharat was a groundbreaking initiative; it was a tectonic shift in Indian healthcare as it ensured that every Indian could avail of quality health facilities without being burdened with financial costs. One must remember that the healthcare landscape was riddled with challenges related to unequal access, lack of affordability, subpar quality of medical services, infrastructure deficits, and funding limitations. While urban areas had somewhat addressed these issues through the emergence of private healthcare institutions, the most vulnerable and underserved populations in remote and rural regions continued to lack access to timely, affordable, and quality medical care.

Hence, in the pursuit of realizing universal health coverage, the Ayushman Bharat Yojana has played a significant role. Regarded as the world's largest government healthcare programme, the initiative focuses on offering three-tier services—primary, secondary, and tertiary care—to citizens.

The Constitution of India emphasized that it was the duty of the state to protect the 'right to health' of all citizens. This commitment included making sure that everyone in every state had free access to healthcare services. However, persistent underfunding in India's healthcare system prevented this goal from being fulfilled. Many government-funded health insurance schemes were started throughout history to improve coverage for particular demographic groups. The National Health Insurance Programme, also known as Rashtriya Swasthya Bima Yojana (RSBY), introduced in 2008, was an important initiative designed to reduce financial risks among lower-income communities. Approximately 41 million families had signed up for RSBY by 2016. Despite this scope, research revealed that the plan did not successfully reduce out-of-pocket costs.[13]

The prime minister grasped the drawbacks and rightly observed, 'Ayushman Bharat Scheme is for the poor, for the middle class and for the common families. We have adopted a holistic approach in our healthcare system. Today our focus is not only on health, but equally on wellness.'[14]

On 23 September 2018, the Government of India took a significant stride towards its ambitious goal of providing quality, affordable, and accessible healthcare for all its residents. In Ranchi, Jharkhand, Prime Minister Modi introduced the Ayushman Bharat-Pradhan Mantri Jan Arogya Yojana (AB-PMJAY), marking a pivotal shift in the nation's healthcare landscape. At the core of Ayushman Bharat's vision lies an unwavering dedication to ensuring that every individual, without exception, receives the medical treatment they are rightfully entitled to. At the launch of the Ayushman Bharat Scheme, PM Modi said, 'We have been listening to the *garibi hatao* [get rid of poverty] slogan, but it was just an attempt to hoodwink the poor. If the [welfare] schemes were implemented, as promised, the poor in the country would have been better off today.'[15]

Under its framework of healthcare delivery, Ayushman Bharat encompasses four pillars:

1. Health and wellness centres (HWCs)
2. Pradhan Mantri Jan Arogya Yojana (PM-JAY)
3. Ayushman Bharat Digital Health Mission (AB-DHM)
4. Pradhan Mantri-Ayushman Bharat Health Infrastructure Mission

Ayushman Bharat emphasizes the delivery of comprehensive primary care through the HWCs, primarily by public healthcare providers. In the Union Budget speech for FY 2018–2019, the HWC programme was announced with a budget of ₹1,200 crore for the flagship programme. To ensure 'Comprehensive Primary Health Care, existing sub-health centres (SHCs) covering a population of 3,000–5,000 were transformed into HWCs. This network was complemented by mobile medical units and other home- and community-based care.

At the SHC level, the HWC is equipped and staffed by an appropriately trained primary healthcare team led by a community health officer, other multi-purpose workers, and accredited social health activists (ASHAs). A primary healthcare centre is linked to a cluster of AB-HWCs at the SHCs, which serves as the first point of referral for many conditions. SHC was also extended to deliver an expanded range of primary healthcare services. The number and qualifications of the staff at primary healthcare centres continue as defined by Indian Public Health Standards.

While this was adopted for the primary healthcare model, a different structure was adopted for secondary and tertiary healthcare—PM-JAY. Since the national health assurance scheme had faltered due to the requirement of funds, PM-JAY expanded its coverage, services, and allocations and worked on monitoring and implementing ModiCare.

PM-JAY provides health coverage to eligible families for hospitalization expenses. The secondary and tertiary care services covered by PM-JAY are delivered through a network of both public and private healthcare providers. This ensures that beneficiaries have access to a wide range of medical facilities and specialists for advanced treatments and interventions.

Addressing the challenges faced by Ayushman Bharat involves navigating a complex landscape of ethical considerations, financial sustainability, healthcare infrastructure, and regulatory frameworks. As India strives to achieve universal health coverage, the Ayushman Bharat initiative emerges as a significant step towards making secondary and tertiary care accessible to a substantial portion of the population while also focusing on strengthening primary healthcare through HWCs. However, the realization of its potential hinges on critical factors such as community engagement, awareness generation, and quality control.

The PM-JAY Advantage

PM-JAY is by many accounts the world's most extensive health assurance initiative, aimed at extending health coverage to ₹5,00,000 per family per year. The coverage encompasses secondary and tertiary care hospitalization, catering to over 10.74 crore underprivileged and vulnerable families and encompassing approximately 50 crore beneficiaries, which constitute the bottom 40 per cent of India's population. The selection of households for inclusion is grounded in the Socio-Economic Caste Census 2011, utilizing deprivation and occupational criteria for rural and urban areas, respectively. PM-JAY operates on full government funding, with implementation costs shared jointly between the central and state governments.[16]

Furthermore, pre-existing medical conditions are encompassed from the time of inception. This implies that any qualifying individual afflicted with a medical condition before inclusion in PM-JAY will have the opportunity to receive treatment for all those pre-existing conditions under this scheme, commencing from the day of enrollment.

For rural residents, the scheme reaches out to those in Scheduled Caste and Scheduled Tribe households, families without male members aged between 16 and 59 years, beggars, and individuals reliant on alms. It also includes families without individuals aged between 16 and 59 years, households with at least one physically challenged member and no able-bodied adult, landless families dependent on manual labour, primitive tribal communities, legally released bonded labourers, families residing in makeshift one-room houses, and those involved in manual scavenging.

In urban areas, the beneficiaries consist of a variety of occupations, including washermen and chowkidars (security guards), ragpickers, mechanics, electricians, repair workers, domestic helpers, sanitation workers, gardeners, and sweepers. The scheme also encompasses home-based artisans, handicraft workers, tailors, cobblers, hawkers, and service providers on streets or pavements. Additionally, plumbers, masons, construction workers, porters, welders, painters, security guards, transport workers like drivers, conductors, helpers, cart or rickshaw pullers, as well as assistants, peons in small establishments, delivery personnel, shopkeepers, and waiters fall under the umbrella of the scheme.[17] This comprehensive list of categories highlights the inclusive nature of the scheme, ensuring that individuals from a wide range of socioeconomic backgrounds in both rural and urban settings have access to essential health coverage.

The testimonials that have emerged since the implementation of the scheme bear testament to its profound impact. It provides families with an adequate buffer from the financial and physiological turmoil that often accompanies unforeseen medical exigencies. In fact, one can argue that beyond the realm of what numerical data says, PM-JAY covers a transformation that is reflected in the lives the programme has touched.

Notably, Prime Minister Modi's involvement ranged from ideation to inauguration of the scheme. His endeavours in promoting the programme, garnering support from diverse stakeholders, and fostering active participation from various states have been instrumental in its resounding success. Moreover, his emphasis on leveraging technology for the transformative advancement of healthcare, as evidenced by initiatives such as the national digital health mission known as Ayushman Bharat Digital Mission (AB-DHM), has brought innovation to the forefront. His recognition of technology's potential to enhance healthcare accessibility, efficiency, and patient outcomes has led to the integration of digital solutions, telemedicine, and robust data management within the healthcare ecosystem.

Ayush Bharat Digital Health Mission[18]

Looking back, it would be fine to say that the COVID-19 pandemic compelled people and governments to embrace digital transformation and rethink prevailing healthcare practices. While the idea of digital public goods was very much in practice in Modi's governance model (UPI, Digital India, JAM, etc.), an adoption of the same for healthcare was limited. In response to the larger digitization and consequent healthcare digitization, PM Modi introduced the AB-DHM in September 2021. The mission's objective is to establish a comprehensive national digital health ecosystem that is well-integrated, efficient, and inclusive.

By employing interoperable frameworks, open protocols, and consent artefacts, this endeavour encourages collaboration among citizens, public and private healthcare providers, digital innovations, and other stakeholders to drive equitable healthcare digitization throughout the country. The National Health Stack was introduced in 2019, adding to the evolving ecosystem for integrated national digital healthcare. Following the same the AB-DHM was introduced which focuses on seven key building blocks. The most important among them is the Ayushman Bharat Health Account, which is a fourteen-digit unique identification number that standardizes an individual's identification process between healthcare providers and facilities.

Earlier, in 2019, during a visit to Jharkhand, Prime Minister Modi engaged with the beneficiaries of the Ayushman Bharat Scheme, which was only a year into implementation then. A poignant moment unfolded as one of the beneficiaries expressed how the scheme had enabled him to undergo essential surgery and, later on, the necessary follow-up treatment. Singing a song in the Nagpuri language (also known as Sadri, spoken in Jharkhand, Bihar, Chattisgarh and Odisha), he eloquently praised the programme's impact. This heartfelt interaction garnered widespread attention, underscored the scheme's significance in transforming lives and echoing the government's commitment to accessible healthcare for millions.[19]

PM Modi also notably tried to affirm the idea of holistic care, wellness and yoga amongst the young and old of India. He has repeatedly spoken about lifestyle diseases and other matters which have an indirect bearing on health care. From pre-natal care to complex life-threatening diseases (60 per cent of health-related deaths occur due to these four diseases: cardiovascular disease, diabetes, respiratory problems, and cancer), there has been intervention on all fronts. The intention of moving from curative to preventive medicine is also laudable and noteworthy.

Not too long ago, I got into a conversation with a middle-aged man from Madhya Pradesh. I was then mulling over the idea of working on a book on public health reforms, so I asked him about what had changed since the days he had seen in his youth. He smiled and said, '*Bahaut change ho gaya hai*' (A lot has changed). He added how the poor in this country did not even have the courage to approach good hospitals for treatment. But now, with cashless services and schemes such as Ayushman Bharat, the vulnerable sections of society have the courage to approach big hospitals and be assured of quality treatment.

Remember the film, *Munna Bhai M.B.B.S.*? The Sanjay Dutt-starrer reached out to so many medical professionals and common hapless citizens across the country when the protagonist asks: '*Agar koi marne waala hai, toh usse form bharna zaroori hai kya?*'

Well, change—real change—has happened due to Prime Minister Modi's initiatives in the healthcare sector. Even Munna Bhai would be impressed!

8

The Cultural Reawakening

'History tells us that powerful people come from powerful places. History was wrong. Powerful people make places powerful.'

These lines from the Kannada blockbuster *KGF* caught the public's imagination soon after the film was released. It was a rage! But, as the internet played its magic, fan-made reels and shorts with footage of Prime Minister Modi were out in no time. Powerful visuals of the prime minister walking was overlayed with some visual transitions and music added on top of it. It made a viral Instagram reel. But, as one looks back, something of a similar kind happened to Varanasi in 2014. Of course, the city was already famed for its religious and spiritual history, but Modi also made it powerful politically.

Kashi/Benaras/Varanasi—whichever name you choose—is perhaps the oldest living city in the world. It is where divinity expresses itself in every word and every action. It is Lord Shiva's favourite place. Kashi is where Tulsidas wrote *Ramcharitmanas* and where Kabir resided. It has one of the twelve Jyotirlingas in Kashi Vishwanath Mandir and a Maha Shakti Peeth at the Manikarnika Ghat. Kashi is where it all ends. And, perhaps, everything begins. Varanasi is revival; Varanasi is restoration.

In the words of Union Minister for Home Affairs, Amit Shah: 'The nine years of the Narendra Modi government have been in a way a "cultural renaissance" for the country.'[1] And this journey began in 2014 when Prime Minister Modi chose Varanasi as his parliamentary constituency. When Modi filed his nomination in 2014, he chose a regular routine event and made it a grand affair. It was, after all, the first time that he was contesting for the Lok Sabha. This, coupled with the fact that the BJP had declared him as its prime ministerial candidate, made the occasion special. The way everyone looked at Varanasi changed. As they say, some people choose an event for grand entries; others enter and make it all grand.

But that was not all. It was the choice of Varanasi (in addition to a constituency in his home state of Gujarat) that grabbed media headlines. There was a political strategy in this. The BJP knew that if it had to win enough seats to form a government in New Delhi, it had to win big in Uttar Pradesh, which contributes eighty seats to the Lok Sabha. Modi, as a candidate from a constituency in this politically crucial state, would spur the party to do well there and also enthuse the party cadre as well as the voters. Not just that, the ripple effect would be felt across the Hindi heartland.

Still, why Varanasi? There were other constituencies in Uttar Pradesh to choose from. It is because Modi, a Shiva devotee, felt a deep spiritual connection with this ancient city. He expressed it when he said that he had not chosen Varanasi on his own, but that Mother Ganga had beckoned him. *'Ma Ganga ne bulaya hai!'*—that one line summed up everything. Of course, he was elected by a thumping margin.

More recently, in an interview with a leading national television channel, Prime Minister Modi got emotional when asked about his connection with Varanasi. He said the relationship went beyond that of an elected representative with his constituents. He was right. His ties with Varanasi reflect his bonds with India's cultural and civilizational history and traditions.

In my view, his decision marked the beginning of a cultural renaissance that was to take place in India. After all, which Indian politician had in the recent past ever commented about a constituency's cultural significance while filing a nomination? A city that transcends time and space, where ancient traditions thrive along with modern values, where the ghats along the Ganga bustle with devotees against the backdrop of many temples, suddenly came alive in the consciousness of millions of Indians.

Modi visited Varanasi for the first time after being anointed the BJP's prime ministerial candidate in December 2013. He did not go directly to the venue where he was to address a public rally. Instead, he visited the iconic Kashi Vishwanath Temple and the Sankatmochan Temple first, seeking the blessings of the gods. In December 2013, in his speech, Modi said he had come from the land of Somnath to take the blessings of Baba Vishwanath.[2]

From that moment until today, when one sees the cultural revolution that has taken place in the hearts and minds of Hindus across the country, there is one person to credit for that: Prime Minister Modi. Whether it's his image of meditating in the Kedarnath cave, taking a dip in the Ganga, scuba diving near Dwarka, or undergoing the various difficult rituals before participating in the consecration ceremony at the Ram Mandir in Ayodhya, Modi has unabashedly worn his faith on his sleeve.

The Gang of Apologetics

Before the Modi era, politicians, more so prime ministers (Vajpayee was an exception), were careful to downplay their religious affiliation, worried that any overt display would compromise their 'secular' credentials. In fact, it had become commonplace for our politicians to even be apologetic about being Hindu. Steeped in the Western concept of secularism, they forgot that dharma was an intrinsic part of India's social and cultural fabric and that the Hindu faith—all-encompassing as it was—wished for no conflict with other faiths; most certainly, it did not seek domination over others. But our politicians would distance themselves from Bharat's glorious culture, be apologetic about it, and also be in denial about our civilizational history and democratic polity. In fact, the little that was done was with the aim to not hurt the sentiment of a certain community. This is reflected in our education system and practices. In effect, starting from the top, the ecosystem filtered down to create a set-up wherein distancing oneself from the Hindu faith rather than proudly owning up to it was the way to sound credible.

Those were the days when Delhi was being ruled over by the 'Lutyens' Zone' or the 'Khan Market Gang'. What suited this 'cabal' was the Nehru–Gandhi family's version of secularism—which meant running down the faith of the country's majority—and that became the gospel truth. Decades after the British colonizers had quit, Indians stayed colonized in their own minds.

Things began to change, and drastically so, with Modi's arrival on the national stage. Which is why his elevation as prime minister is such an important development. Over the last decade, Modi has taken several initiatives that aim to revive and restore India's cultural glory. Policies and initiatives have been undertaken for the restoration and development of cultural festivals. The reconstruction and redevelopment of ancient temples and the introduction of initiatives, such as the Char Dham Yatra, among others, have served to strengthen the new reawakening. The Char Dham Mahamarg Vikas Pariyojana project is a pilgrim circuit in the Himalayas that connects four prominent pilgrimage spots (Gangotri, Yamunotri, Kedarnath, and Badrinath) in Uttarakhand.

Prime Minister Modi's spiritual association with the Himalayan state is old. When Kedarnath was devastated by floods in 2013, he was the chief minister of Gujarat. He was one of the first few people to conduct a survey and offer help to the chief minister of Uttarakhand, who was from the Congress party. Medical and make-shift accommodation facilities came up in no time, and authorities from Gujarat were on the ground to assist in every manner. It is a different matter that the state government, under pressure from the Congress-led UPA government at the Centre, refused to formally accept his help. But people in Uttarakhand remember that phase vividly and recall how Modi had arrived in Dehradun in no time. His pace and scale surprised everyone. Perhaps, the experience he had gained in managing natural calamities in Gujarat, such as the Machhu Dam-Morbi disaster or the Bhuj earthquake helped him.

Then, there is PRASAD (Pilgrimage Rejuvenation and Spiritual Augmentation Drive), a scheme that aims to develop and beautify pilgrimage destinations across India by improving infrastructure, facilities, and services at select sites. Places such as Varanasi have experienced tremendous all-round development. The creation of the Kashi Vishwanath Corridor in Varanasi and the Mahakal Lok Corridor in Ujjain marked a cultural rejuvenation that blended the old with the new. While the total cost of the Mahakal project is estimated at more than ₹850 crore, that of the Varanasi project is close to ₹800 crore. As part of the overall plan, more than forty ancient temples were restored and beautified. More than 75,000 devotees can be accommodated in the new Kashi Vishwanath temple complex.

The showcasing of our heritage is at the heart of the cultural renaissance. At the inauguration of the Mahakal Corridor, Modi pointed out that such projects were an expression of freedom from the mentality of slavery and a demonstration of pride in our heritage. He said that several foreign invaders had attempted to destroy the spiritual energy of cities, such as Ujjain, but in vain.

The New Bharat

The above-mentioned projects are some of the many initiatives that signify the rise of Bharat and how Modi is leading the charge. While reclaiming the lost glory is one part of the endeavour, branding it is another. Prime Minister Modi is the brand ambassador of this new Bharat. Visuals of him—while performing the rituals on the Ram Mandir idol consecration or praying at Kashi Vishwanath, Mahakal in Ujjain, or the many temples spread across the country—have struck a chord in the hearts of millions of Indians and made them feel proud of Sanatana Dharma.

It is a matter of record that the footfalls in both Varanasi and Ayodhya have increased exponentially; in the first case, after the inauguration of the temple corridor, and in the second, after the consecration ceremony at the grand Ram Mandir. More and more people are learning about our cultural past, identifying with it, and taking pride in it.

Of course, the increased number of visitors has been facilitated by an enhancement in connectivity. The road network that has come up in India in the last ten years is a never-before-seen feat. The Char Dham highway is a case in point. A larger railway network and fast trains have increased accessibility to the pilgrim spots. With more airports, different cities in India are more connected than ever before. A family can now take the fast Vande Bharat Express or opt for air travel to Varanasi. Similarly, Ayodhya is now connected to major cities in the country by air.

*

This brings us to the Ram Mandir in Ayodhya, for it continues to draw our attention months after the high-profile consecration ceremony was conducted. The Vishwa Hindu Parishad started a movement for the construction of a Ram temple in the 1980s. By 1990, the movement had gathered enough traction for the BJP to organize the Ram Rath Yatra to reclaim the birthplace of Lord Ram. A large campaign was started to that effect, galvanizing a huge section of the Hindu population of the country. Narendra Modi was then an organization man for the BJP and played an important role in organizing the yatra. There are pictures of him with the late L.K. Advani, who led the yatra, from those days.

For the next three decades, the Ram Mandir issue was discussed in the courts, in the media, and among the intelligentsia. Even while this was going on, the BJP continued working on it, declaring its support for the temple in all its election manifestos. It was mentioned in the party's 2014 manifesto as well, and its commitment was visible to all. On the other hand, opposing parties refused to extend support to the construction of a temple on the (then disputed) site. Instead, they went out of their way to appease Muslims by regularly expressing their opposition to the construction of the temple.

The naysayers in the Opposition also argued that the mention of a Ram temple at Ayodhya in the BJP's manifesto was merely an electoral stunt by the party to garner the majority community's votes. Opposition leaders taunted the BJP by saying: '*Mandir wahiin banayenge, par tareekh nahin batayenge*' (You say that you will build the temple there, but do not give the date).

That taunt lost its sell-by date after the Supreme Court ruled in favour of the Hindu side. A non-political trust was created to handle the construction of the Ram temple and establish a deadline for the completion of the construction's first phase, after which a Ram idol could be placed inside the sanctum sanctorum. Much to the chagrin of the Opposition, the temple was built according to schedule, and the consecration ceremony was held. The trust issued invitations to prominent political leaders from the Opposition, but they refused to attend.

The day of 22 January 2024 will be remembered as a golden day in India's cultural history, for it was on that day that the temple was inaugurated by Prime Minister Modi, and the Ram Lalla idol was consecrated. Thousands of people had gathered in Ayodhya, from common devotees to celebrities. A festive and electric atmosphere prevailed, and people, including religious leaders—many of whom had campaigned for decades for the construction of the temple and had all but lost hope of seeing it happen in their lifetime—danced and sang. There were also tears of joy. Even the celebrities could not remain unaffected by the spontaneous outburst of happiness. Many were moved, and they had no words to express their feelings.

Prime Minister Modi went on the offensive thereafter, castigating the political leaders for their boycott. His arguments hit home. He also used their petty refusal as an election plank, and it resonated with the people.

Earlier, at another high-profile event, he inaugurated the Mahakaleshwar Jyotirlinga in Ujjain. In 2017, he unveiled the 112-foot-tall Lord Adiyogi statue in Coimbatore. He inaugurated the Somnath seaside promenade. The prime minister also laid the foundation stone for a redeveloped temple in Kalika Mata. In 2024, he launched the Kamakhya Divyalok Pariyojana.

From the plains of Varanasi and Ujjain to the mountains of Kedarnath—only a leap of faith can take the mind that far. There is one thing common among the three places: they all celebrate Lord Shiva. Modi is a Shiva devotee, so how could he ignore Kedarnath, where an ancient Shiva temple stands in resplendent isolation, with snow-capped peaks forming the background? After taking over as prime minister in 2014, Modi resolved to redevelop Kedarnath and its neighbouring areas. The idea was to make the sacred site more accessible to pilgrims and assorted visitors, provide them with the amenities needed, and enhance safety measures in and around Kedarnath.

In 2017, after offering prayers, he studied a presentation made by Uttarakhand's officials on the redevelopment of the region. He liked what he saw and added some of his own suggestions. The presentation gave proposals to prevent major damages in the eventuality of floods and other natural calamities, round-the-clock power supply, and construction of homes for the resident priest and guests. Modi also laid the foundation stones for as many as five redevelopment projects. Work began in earnest thereafter; needless to add, the prime minister gave strict instructions that work had to be completed as per the deadline agreed upon. Today, Kedarnath bears a new look, with visible all-round improvement.

Modi's determination to glorify the Sanatana spirit has taken him beyond the borders of India. He inaugurated a huge Swaminarayan temple in, of all places, Abu Dhabi. It is the first stone temple in the UAE. The temple was constructed by the Bochasanwasi Shri Akshar Purushottam Swaminarayan Sanstha (BAPS) on a 27-acre site in Abu Mureikhah, near Al Rahba off the Dubai-Abu Dhabi Sheikh Zayed Highway, at a cost of around ₹700 crore. The grand ceremony witnessed the participation of nearly 5,000 people. And, in Bahrain, another Islamic nation, he initiated the revamp of a 200-year-old temple.

Modi loses no opportunity to showcase India's rich culture. He showed a remarkable sense of proactiveness in getting back Hindu idols that had gone missing from India and were discovered in foreign lands. BJP leader Anil Baluni wrote in August 2023, 'One of the important outcomes of Prime Minister Narendra Modi's state visit to the US was the decision by the Biden administration to return over 105 ancient statues and antiquities to India, which were smuggled out of the country. Of these, two 12th-century statues—Lord Shiva's rare Lingodbhava statue and Bodhisattva Manjushri statue—have already reached India.'[3]

PM Modi has a wonderful understanding of the importance of symbols to drive home the point of our cultural history. He proved that with the ceremonial installation of the Sengol in the new Parliament House. The Sengol is a gold-plated, silver sceptre that was originally gifted to Jawaharlal Nehru by a Tamil *adheenam* (priest) at a religious ceremony on the evening of Independence in 1947. It is considered a sacred symbol of fair and equitable governance. After that, the sceptre was all but forgotten and supposedly consigned to a museum, marked as Nehru's walking stick! PM Modi decided to adopt the Sengol as a national symbol of *Amrit Kaal*, which the nation was celebrating.

Spirituality, religion, and history—they all combine to make the Sengol so special. The spirit of 15 August 1947, the promise of hope and optimism, and a determination to build a stronger and more prosperous India are all inculcated in the sceptre.

Faith for All to See

Modi's first visit as prime minister to the US coincided with the Navaratri festival. Says a report, "PM Narendra Modi will begin his annual ritual of 'nakkoda' fasting that he has been observing every navratri for the past 35 years — nine days of drinking only water and strict adherence to yoga, meditation and puja at dusk..."[4] Prime Minister Modi kept his fast throughout the visit, much to the admiration of his hosts. It also became news all over the world! One wonders when was the last time that the ritual of a Hindu leader was spoken about this extensively in the press?

While the media went gaga, Modi himself was unmoved; for him, the fast was simply an expression of his deep-rooted belief in Sanatana Dharma, a personal act that was as natural as it was mandatory in his view.

It set off a cascade reaction, where the ordinary Hindu did not feel odd to fast or make their dietary restrictions known during a religious period. It had become, until then, almost a normal thing to disregard the sentiments of a Hindu taking dietary precautions during Navaratri. Snide remarks would be passed, even in their presence. Strict vegetarianism was being looked upon by the so called 'elites' of Delhi. The passive aggression worked when one began hearing of stories of next generation Arya Samajis being fine with non-vegetarian food.

Contrast this with the respect that was accorded to others who fasted during Ramzan and the rush of political leaders of all hues to register their presence for Iftar and you will understand what I am saying. The double standards were vivid. But that was perhaps the way of the world. Coexisting with some fear and evolving habits to exist (or maybe, live).

The common Hindu began to notice nuances that were earlier ignored. For example, when a friend of mine visited Wayanad, she came back with stories of how almost every house in the region had a picture of Jesus on their front doors or verandahs. There were mosques all around, and the Hindu identity was as good as missing in the area. Like her, many Hindus had begun to realize that the stories of rampant conversions that we heard were not vivid imaginations of the RSS and the like; they had actually happened and were happening. It's just that Bharat is culturally now more awake and has begun talking about them with a greater level of assertiveness.

Today, a Hindu proudly wears a *kalava*. News anchors sport it, sportspersons wear it, actors flaunt it, and so does the common Sanatani Hindu. Temple visits are more frequent and done in full-camera view. How has this become possible? Because Modi showed the way. There has been a renewed interest in reviving and preserving traditional Hindu practices, such as yoga, Ayurveda, and Vedic rituals. The government's support for these ancient traditions has contributed to a cultural reawakening among Hindus.

Efforts have been made to reclaim and highlight India's Sanatana heritage. This has fostered a sense of pride in and connection with the country's rich cultural history, especially among the Hindus, but also among sections of Muslims and others. The government has promoted the study and dissemination of the Sanskrit language and Hindu scriptures, encouraging a deeper understanding of Hindu philosophy, literature, and spirituality. Initiatives have been introduced to incorporate Hindu cultural education into school curricula, ensuring that younger generations are exposed to and knowledgeable about their cultural heritage.

PM Modi's 'gift diplomacy' (where he presents foreign dignitaries gifts that represent India's rich cultural heritage) represents a strategic and culturally resonant approach to diplomatic engagement.

Rather than opting for generic or impersonal gifts, Modi selects items that are deeply rooted in Indian tradition, history, and craftsmanship. For instance, during his visits abroad, Modi has often presented handcrafted items, such as traditional Indian textiles, artefacts, and artworks.

Modi's choice of gifts often carries symbolic significance, tailored to resonate with the recipient's interests or the bilateral agenda. For example, during his visit to Japan, Modi presented Prime Minister Shinzo Abe with a specially curated selection of Indian tea varieties, underscoring the shared appreciation for tea culture between the two nations. Similarly, during meetings with leaders from African countries, Modi has gifted replicas of the Ashoka Chakra—a symbol of peace, progress, and cooperation—symbolizing India's commitment to supporting Africa's developmental goals.

Whether it is presenting copies of ancient Indian manuscripts to world leaders or gifting solar panels to promote clean energy cooperation, Modi's gifts often carry messages of innovation, sustainability, and cultural heritage, aligning with India's broader diplomatic objectives.

The cultural awakening hence observed under PM Modi's regime reflects a complex interplay of historical, political, and sociocultural factors that is shaping contemporary India. And, it all effectively converges into the five resolves—the *Panch Pran* of *Amrit Kaal*—for 2047 that he spoke about from the ramparts of the Red Fort in his 15 August 2022 speech: the goal of a developed India, to remove any trace of colonial mindset, be proud of our roots, unity, and sense of duty among citizens.[5]

Conclusion

In 2024, while the election season was on, I mulled over many questions on how Prime Minister Modi had proved to be different from other leaders. What makes him special? What provokes the voters to be attracted by him? How is it that he has acquired a halo around him? There are pragmatic reasons, but there is also the emotional element. The answer perhaps lies somewhere in between these two.

Modi became the prime minister after spending around fifteen years in the RSS, some fifteen years as a BJP organization man, and close to twelve years as the chief minister of Gujarat. He came to the country's high office, therefore, with much experience, both in the organization and as an administrator. As a Sangh swayamsevak, he understood the pulse of the people. He also came to appreciate the country's rich cultural and civilizational values and the need to protect and promote them.

Through organizational work within the party, he learnt to manage power equations and ensure a firm grip on the party's functioning. During his chief ministerial days, he understood the art of governance. His résumé, by all accounts, had been impressive. He was also ahead of his time for he documented his journey very well. Add to this, his personal integrity and out-of-the-box ways of working. He does not forget or leave behind the people who helped him through his journey. Hence, everyone who has in any capacity worked with Narendra Modi has the ability to perform marches alongside him.

From a practical and political point of view, he emerged as the sole choice of voters in 2014 for the prime ministership. He trumped the Opposition like few others had done before him. Even a decade later, his charisma remains intact, and his hold over the party and the government is as firm as earlier. While the BJP has had presidents during his tenure as the head of the government, his stamp on the party's functioning is evident. It was riding on his personal stature that the party has notched success after success. However, it is important to note here that the achievements of his government since 2014 have played a major role in the electoral victories, complementing his personal charisma.

A shift happened since he assumed power. For some time, India was troubled by a development deficit. Political speeches were aplenty, such as *Garibi Hatao*. Many promises were made at election rallies. A friend once said, '*Bhashanon se sarkar banti thi aur chalti thi*' (Governments were formed and run by speeches). This needed to change. But who was to bring it? The ecosystem was such that whatever crumbs the electorate got were accepted as a blessing. Year after year, the middle class in India would sit in front of their television and radio sets to listen to the budget speech, hoping for some respite from tax burdens. Governments were formed and run by a select few. There was a socialist mindset, but the tenets of socialism were not practised. Leaders made grand speeches, promising a socialist way of functioning, but they promoted crony capitalism and the criminalization of politics. A coterie ruled the country.

The prevalent system needed mending, and urgently! Prime Minister Modi grasped the fundamentals, which were to improve the lives of the poor, the underprivileged, and the marginalized. That is where the work had to begin because they were the ones who had paid the heaviest price for the failures and hypocrisies of the leaders. These people needed quality medical care that was affordable, decent housing, cooking gas connections, toilets, electricity, tap water connections, and more. They needed good roads and dependable transportation. Seventy years of independence had not given them these basic necessities in the adequate measures that were required—or, in some cases, not at all.

PM Modi understood that once the essentials were made available, a sense of empowerment would grip the people and make them confident and capable of turning their lives for the better. All he had to do was to be the catalyst. This he could do by implementing targeted social welfare measures, reviving the economy, revamping the health and education systems, and launching a rapid pace of infrastructure development.

The initiatives thereafter resulted in the evolution of a new class of voter-beneficiaries. Until that happened, most electoral calculations revolved around caste arithmetic. Poll strategists, belonging to various political parties, and psephologists based their projections on the caste metric as if little else mattered. Admittedly, in the earlier days, perhaps little else mattered. But changes began to happen over the last decade, with the rise of the beneficiary class that cut across caste divisions. People who happened to be connected with the grassroots and interacted with those on the ground felt the change, whereas those seated in air-conditioned rooms and making their projections premised on old realities missed the whiff of transformation in the mood of the people. Only they could have been taken by surprise over the 2019 Lok Sabha results, when the BJP romped home with a bigger win than in 2014.

*

In January 2019, I was in Jind and happened to be at an important election meeting of the BJP. It promised to be an intense election, just a few months before the 2019 Lok Sabha polls. Even more, it was a by-election that, in hindsight, set forth the BJP campaign in the state. In the meeting, however, an important list was discussed. The workers had in their possession a list of people who had benefitted from the various schemes of the government. The party workers were asked to reach out to them. A call centre was also established to contact the beneficiaries. Now, imagine this drive being played out all over the country. The message was obvious: Give people real and tangible benefits, and they will come out to vote for you. It was the arrival of a new class of voters.

Nobody is saying that caste as a determinant has ceased to matter in Indian elections. It is there, deep-seated and deep-rooted. My forefathers battled this cause over a century ago, with my family continuing to work on the ground with the same spirit. The results of the 2024 general election, in a way, are a demonstration of the stranglehold the caste factor still has on the country's politics. However, it is also now a fact that when governance delivers and that delivery converts into demonstrable benefits for the people, it reflects more than before in electoral outcomes. One sure way to judge good governance is the country's economic health.

Kunal Sen, from United Nations University, wrote in May 2024,

> If one was to go by economic growth figures alone, the Modi government's performance has been impressive. When Modi came to power in 2014, economic growth was sluggish. A series of high-profile corruption cases led to a loss of investor confidence in the Indian economy. But between 2014 and 2022, India's gross domestic product (GDP) per capita (a measure

> of income per head) rose from US$5,000 (£4,000) to over US$7,000—an increase of roughly 40% in eight years. These calculations use purchasing power parity, a way of comparing general purchasing power over time and between countries.[1]

Further, according to a Brookings Report, India has also eliminated 'extreme poverty'.

As mentioned earlier, Prime Minister Modi has invested heavily in transport infrastructure over the years. For example, Indian Railways has undergone a remarkable metamorphosis. Strategic investments and increased budgetary allocations have resulted in over 25,000 kilometres of new railway tracks being laid, surpassing the total length found in many developed countries. Railway electrification surged to 94 per cent, and unmanned rail crossings have been eliminated. The government has also introduced other measures, such as GPS-based tracking systems and bio-toilets, making travel safer and convenient. Further, the government has pushed ahead with the dedicated freight corridor and introduced semi-high-speed trains, such as Vande Bharat and Namo Bharat.

Over 55,000 kilometres of highways have been constructed in the last decade, alongside some noteworthy projects, such as the Bharatmala Pariyojana. The Modi government has also prioritized multi-modal connectivity through initiatives such as the PM Gati Shakti Yojana and the National Infrastructure Pipeline. With Sagarmala, India's vast coastline is being optimally leveraged for the first time.

With the Ude Desh ka Aam Nagrik (UDAN) project, the number of airports in the country has doubled and regional connectivity improved. The Smart Cities mission aims to develop 100 selected cities into 'smart cities'. Along with it, an expanding metro network is proving to be a game-changer in urban transportation.

While economic growth is important, equally critical is the country's internal security ecosystem. If national security considerations are not taken care of, neither economic nor social development is sustainable. Our borders have to be adequately protected and internal disturbances have to be nipped in the bud. The Modi government has shown the door to the appeasement policy of earlier regimes. The near-daily incidents of violence in Jammu and Kashmir (stone-pelting, etc), and the Maoist terror has been contained to a large extent. The success could be attributed to the 'whole-of-government' approach and better cooperation and coordination between different agencies. Numbers suggest that between 2004 and 2014, the number of violent incidents was 33,000; between 2014 and 2023, this came down by 62 per cent to 12,466. The total number of deaths among civilians and security forces in such incidents has declined by 72 per cent from 11,900 to 3,276.

The Modi government showed remarkable courage and conviction by abolishing Article 370 and Article 35A, thus fully integrating Jammu and Kashmir with the whole of India. These provisions in the Constitution had tied the hands of the union governments in dealing effectively with separatist elements in the region, and also in bringing development to the required levels to the people of Jammu and Kashmir. Besides, these articles had been an impediment in delivering social justice to the residents of the region—for instance, reservations available to certain communities across the country did not apply to similar communities in Jammu and Kashmir due to the presence of Article 370. It was not an easy decision to take; no previous government had dared to scrap the provision.

Weeks before the Modi government took the bold move, regional leaders had issued all kinds of threats in case the provision was done away with. They said that Kashmir would burn, that there would be none in the region who would hold the Indian tricolour high. But nothing of the sort happened. The government ensured through preventive measures that Kashmir remained peaceful. Today, many have come around to admit that the region is better off without Article 370, that peace has returned, and that democratic development has gained firm roots there.

The restive Northeast too has been taken care of. The Modi government has signed over nine peace agreements in the region, under which more than 9,000 youth have given up arms and joined the mainstream. The union government has worked to resolve border, racial, and religious disputes in the Northeast, working closely with the elected governments of the different states. The Armed Forces (Special Powers) Act (AFSPA) has been lifted from more than 70 per cent of the region—an indication of the restoration of normalcy. The northeastern states have seen an unprecedented level of developmental activities, and there has been a union minister tasked especially with the affairs of the region.

The Modi government's zero-tolerance policy on terrorism has not only been visible but also borne fruit. Vigil on the borders has been enhanced and the government has given a free hand to our armed forces personnel to deal with ground situations as they deem fit. Thus, while we did not hesitate to strike inside Pakistan to deliver a firm message that terrorism against India would no longer be tolerated, our forces also hit out strongly against Chinese aggression along the Line of Actual Control. Towards this approach, the Modi government has launched a drive to modernize our armed forces and also reduce their dependency on the import of warfare equipment—the indigenous drive has begun to show results.

There is no domain of governance that does not have the Modi imprint. He has given some reason or the other for people to vote for him. Whether it outweighs other considerations at polls is a subject of another conversation. For now, Pradhan Mantri Narendra Damodardas Modi has been voted back to power for his third term as the prime minister of the world's largest democracy. This is no small achievement, given that many important world leaders have been going southward in their popularity ratings.

Albeit with a reduced majority, the NDA he leads has begun working on its ambitious plan to make India a developed nation—Viksit Bharat—by 2047, when we celebrate 100 years of our independence.

Notes

Preface

1 https://economictimes.indiatimes.com/news/politics-and-nation/disruptor-in-chief-is-not-modi-but-the-people-of-india-pm-modi/articleshow/57707303.cms?from=mdr

Chapter 1. The Modi Phenomenon: Before and After

1 Kingshuk Nag, *The Saffron Tide* (New Delhi: Rupa Publications India Pvt. Ltd., 2014), p. 78.

2 Modi began his schooling from Jethalal Joshi's Gamthi Shala, school behind his house up to Clas IV. He completed upper primary class (Class V-VII) from No. 1 Primary School commonly known as Durbar. For classes VIII-XI he joined Bhagvatacharya Narayanacharya High School. For higher edcation he moved to MN College at Visnagar, about 30 minutes from Vadnagar by train.

3 Paavani Sinha and Nikita Parmar, *Being Modi* (New Delhi: Vitasta Publishing Pvt. Ltd., 2014).

4 Not many know that Modi had a 'prasadi' flower in his jacket pocket when he took oath as the prime minister on 26 May 2014. It had arrived along with a letter addressing him as Narendrabhai, from Swami Atmasthananda in Belur Math.

5 'The Monk Who Changed Narendra Modi's Life', *The Daily Star*, 29 April 2015, https://www.thedailystar.net/world/the-monk-who-changed-narendra-modi's-life-80468.

6 'Modi Wanted to be Ramakrishna Monk, Rejected Thrice', *The Times of India*, 9 April 2013, https://timesofindia.indiatimes.com/city/kolkata/

modi-wanted-to-be-ramakrishna-monk-rejected-thrice/articleshow/19468165.cms.

7 Kishor Makwana, *Modi: Common Man's PM* (New Delhi: Prabhat Prakashan, 2020).

8 Ajay Singh argues that it was in February–March 1987 that Modi was made GS (Organisation) of the state unit. The official website puts the date to 3 February 1987.

9 Kishor Makwana, *Modi: Common Man's PM* (New Delhi: Prabhat Prakashan, 2020), p. 127.

10 Ajay Singh, *The Architect of the New BJP: How Narendra Modi Transformed the Party* (New Delhi: Penguin Random House India, 2022), p. 24.

11 Ibid., p. 25.

12 Ibid., p. 27

13 Narendra Modi, 'Timeline', Official Website of Prime Minister Narendra Modi, accessed on 3 August 2024.

14 Ajay Singh, *The Architect of the New BJP*, p. 29.

15 Ibid., p. 30.

16 https://www.youtube.com/watch?v=hIuuVYjui5k

17 https://www.youtube.com/watch?v=hIuuVYjui5k

18 Andy Marino, *Narendra Modi: A Political Biography* (New Delhi: HarperCollins, 2014).

19 Ibid.

20 Ibid.

21 Praful Bidwai, 'The Politics of Fear', Rediff News, 28 September 2005. https://www.rediff.com/news/2005/sep/28bidwai.htm.

22 Andy Marino, *Narendra Modi: A Political Biography*.

23 Ibid.

24 Ibid.

Chapter 3. Crafting a New Sports Ecosystem

1 Narendra Modi, 'Sports Now a Serious Career Option', T*he Times of India*, 27 May 2017, https://timesofindia.indiatimes.com/sports/more-sports/others/sports-now-a-serious-career-option-narendra-modi/articleshow/59164275.cms.

2 Ibid.

3 Ashim Roy, 'Games and Sports in Ancient India', *International Education and Research Journal* 3, no. 5 (May 2017): 1-4, E-ISSN 2454-9916.

4 V. Venkata Rao, 'Who Invented the Board Game Snakes and Ladders?' *The Times of India*, 3 April 2009, https://timesofindia.indiatimes.com/who-invented-the-board-game-snakes-and-ladders/articleshow/3585003.cms.

5 'Field Hockey: Who Has Enjoyed Most Success at the Olympics?' Olympics.com, 22 June 2021, https://olympics.com/en/news/field-hockey-who-has-enjoyed-most-success-at-the-olympics.

6 'India at the Olympics: History, Medals, Athletes, Performance, Results, and Position', Olympics.com, https://olympics.com/en/news/india-olympics-history-medals-athletes-performance-results-position.

7 Chandresh Narayanan, *75 Years of Indian Sports* (New Delhi: Rupa Publications, 2022).

8 Kiren Rijiju, 'Kiren Rijiju Appeals to Sports Federations to Stop Infighting Causing Harm to Athletes', 1 December 2019, *The Bridge*, https://thebridge.in/news/kiren-rijiju-appeals-sports-federations-stop-infighting-causing-harm-athletes/?infinitescroll=1.

9 'Manipur to Get India's First Sports University', NDTV, 23 May 2018, https://www.ndtv.com/india-news/manipur-to-get-india-first-sports-university-1861296.

10 Bharatiya Janata Party, BJP Manifesto 2014, https://www.bjp.org/bjp-manifesto-2014.

11 'Government of India Launches National Sports Talent Search Scheme', Press Information Bureau, 5 January 2016, https://pib.gov.in/newsite/PrintRelease.aspx?relid=158442.

12 'Narendra Modi's Charm Bowls over Asian Games Medallists', NDTV Sports, 2 October 2014, https://sports.ndtv.com/asian-games-2014/narendra-modi-s-charm-bowls-over-asian-games-medallists-1511277.

13 '103 Individual Athletes and 2 Hockey Teams Selected as Core Group under the TOPS', Press Information Bureau,

16 March 2023, https://pib.gov.in/PressReleasePage.aspx?PRID=1942494.

14 Narendra Modi (@narendramodi), 'Tweet', Twitter, 1 August 2023, https://twitter.com/narendramodi/status/1688919446264725504.

15 '"He Didn't Make Us Feel We Were Talking to PM": P.R. Sreejesh on Interaction with Modi', News18, 2 August 2023, accessed on 3 August 2024, https://www.news18.com/news/sports/he-didnt-make-us-feel-we-were-talking-to-pm-pr-sreejesh-on-interaction-with-modi-4096820.html.

16 '"Talking with PM Modi Gives Us Motivation to Do Better": Para Table Tennis Star Bhavina Patel', *The Times of India*, 13 August 2022, accessed on 3 August 2024, https://timesofindia.indiatimes.com/sports/more-sports/others/talking-with-pm-modi-gives-us-motivation-to-do-better-para-table-tennis-star-bhavina-patel/articleshow/93544277.cms.

17 'P.R. Sreejesh Recalls His Interaction with PM Modi: "He Spoke in Friendly Manner and Took Us in Our Comfort Zone"', *Times Now News*, accessed on 3 August 2024, 2 August 2023, https://www.timesnownews.com/sports/others/article/pr-sreejesh-recalls-his-interaction-with-pm-modi-he-spoke-in-friendly-mannerand-took-us-in-our-comfort-zone/800685.

18 The Modi Story (@themodistory), 'Tweet', Twitter, 8 May 2023, https://twitter.com/themodistory/status/1655129528791076864.

Chapter 4. Leave No One Behind

1 Mana Stars, Exclusive Video: IAF Wing Commander Abhinandan Varthaman is Safe In Pakistan Custody, https://www.youtube.com/watch?v=L9cepFe0QRs&t=22s

2 'Our Nuclear Weapons are Not for Diwali: PM Modi on Pak's Nuclear Button Threat', *India Today*, 21 April 2019, https://www.indiatoday.in/elections/lok-sabha-2019/story/

our-nuclear-weapons-are-not-for-diwali-pm-modi-on-pak-nuclear-button-threat-1506893-2019-04-21.

3 'A Rare Phone Call, Secret Letter: How India Got Pak to Release IAF's Abhinandan', *Hindustan Times*, 27 February 2021, https://www.hindustantimes.com/india-news/a-rare-phone-call-secret-letter-how-india-got-pak-to-release-iaf-s-abhinandan-101614411836282.html.

4 'Abhinandan, Wing Commander, to Be Released Tomorrow as Peace Gesture: Pak PM Imran Khan', *Indian Express*, February 28, 2019, https://indianexpress.com/article/pakistan/abhinandan-wing-commander-to-be-released-tomorrow-as-peace-gesture-pak-pm-imran-khan-5605149/.

5 Verinder Grover, *Africa and India's Foreign Policy* (New Delhi: Deep and Deep Publications, 1992).

6 Mehta, Jagat S. 'Negotiating Compensation for Indians with Idi Amin's Government.' *India International Centre Quarterly* 28, no. 3 (2001): 25–46. http://www.jstor.org/stable/23005558.

7 'For Thousands of Indians, Gulf Crisis Becomes a Nightmare Without End', *India Today*, 30 September 1990, accessed on 3 August 2024, https://www.indiatoday.in/magazine/special-report/story/19900930-for-thousands-of-indians-gulf-crisis-becomes-a-nightmare-without-end-813091-1990-09-29.

8 Ibid.

9 'China to Send Troops to Help Pakistan Combat Militants,' Reuters, 21 July 2009, https://www.reuters.com/article/idUSSGE72101Z/.

10 Ibid.

11 'Indian Aid Worker Freed by Taliban After 8 Months; Modi Delighted,' *Business Standard*, 23 February 2015, https://www.business-standard.com/article/news-ians/indian-aid-worker-freed-by-taliban-after-8-months-modi-delighted-roundup-115022300009_1.html.

12 Ibid.

13 'Was an ISIS Hostage: A Kerala Nurse's Iraq Diary', NDTV, 10 June 2015, https://www.ndtv.com/blog/i-was-an-isis-hostage-a-kerala-nurses-iraq-diary-593731.

14 The Economic Times: Business News, Personal Finance, Financial News, India Stock Market Investing, Economy News, *The Economic Times*, https://economictimes.indiatimes.com/defaultinterstitial.cms.

15 'Saddam Hussain Connection Likely Helped in Nurses' Release from Iraq', *The Economic Times*, 30 June 2014, https://economictimes.indiatimes.com/news/politics-and-nation/saddam-hussien-connection-likely-helped-in-nurses-release-from-iraq/articleshow/37917551.cms?from=mdr.

16 DeshGujaratHD, Sushma Swaraj on Operation Rahat in Yemen; PM Modi mentioned it recently, https://www.youtube.com/watch?v=Qkau5oHcPpM

17 Dr S. Jaishankar, Interview with External Affairs Minister of India, YouTube, https://www.youtube.com/watch?v=RFm-EimAQIA&t=1788s.

18 'PM Modi's Personal Call to Wuhan Evacuated Kashmiri Student Nizam | COVID-19', Mirrow Now, https://www.youtube.com/watch?v=y4EjbjfnId8

19 Aaj Tak, 'Operation Ganga' को लेकर S Jaishankar ने संसद में क्या कुछ कहा? | Latest News, https://www.youtube.com/watch?v=ayE0RTbVgIk

20 'Pakistani Student Thanks Indian PM Modi for Rescuing Her from Ukraine,' WION, March 1, 2022, https://www.youtube.com/watch?v=xGwuQtDBXA8.

21 'Full Text of Jaishankar's Address at St. Stephen's Alumni Annual Lecture', The Print, 18 December 2021, https://theprint.in/india/full-text-of-jaishankars-address-at-st-stephens-alumni-annual-lecture/889794/.

22 Blukraft. *Modi@20 (New Delhi: Blukraft Publications, 2022).*

23 'PM Modi Hai Toh Mumkin Hai: Evacuees after Reaching Delhi from Crisis-Hit Sudan', *The Economic Times*, 1 May 2023, https://economictimes.indiatimes.com/news/india/

pm-modi-hai-toh-mumkin-hai-evacuees-after-reaching-delhi-from-crisis-hit-sudan/articleshow/99947156.cms?from=mdr.

Chapter 5. Global Diplomacy: Both Assertive and Humanitarian

1 https://www.businesstoday.in/latest/economy/story/indias-monthly-oil-purchase-from-russia-less-than-europes-in-an-afternoon-jaishankar-329481-2022-04-12
2 https://twitter.com/ani/status/1513650068594704387?s=61&t=GKq3d9xK1NF-daQ6DRwq0uQ
3 https://www.thehindu.com/news/national/in-a-first-modi-invites-saarc-leaders-for-his-swearingin/article6033710.ece
4 Blukraft. *Modi@20 (New Delhi: Blukraft Publications, 2022).*
5 Ibid.
6 https://twitter.com/narendramodi/status/1770427197456634364?s=61&t=t5NKf8Mm49CErENtxTvRfA

Chapter 6. New Narrative in Writing and Films

1 https://franpritchett.com/00generallinks/macaulay/txt_minute_education_1835.html
2 https://www.youtube.com/watch?v=QVUS8Dv04mo&t=5s

Chapter 7. Affordable and Humane Healthcare

1 Jyoti Thottam, 'Six Nuns Came to India to Start a Hospital. They Ended Up Changing a Country', *New York Times, 2 April 2022,* accessed on 3 August 2024, https://www.nytimes.com/2022/04/02/opinion/india-nuns-nurses-hospital.html.
2 'History of Cochin Royal Family', Cochin Royal History, accessed on 3 August 2024, https://www.cochinroyalhistory.org/pages.php?menu_id=2&submenu_id=5&submenu2_id=17
3 https://www.livemint.com/news/india/a-short-history-of-indian-economy-1947 2019-tryst-with-destiny-other-stories-1565801528109.html
4 Rao, K. Sujatha, *Do We Care? India's Health System* (New Delhi: Oxford University Press, 2017).

5 'BJP's Manifesto 2014', Bharatiya Janata Party, accessed on 3 August 2024, https://www.bjp.org/bjp-manifesto-2014.

6 https://www.indiatoday.in/india/story/modi-make-in-india-healthcare-digital-mumbai-pm-clean-neonatal-maternal-mortality-224540-2014-10-25

7 'PM Modi Pitches for "Make in India" in Healthcare, Digital India in Mumbai', *India Today, 25* October 2014, accessed on 3 August 2024, https://www.indiatoday.in/india/story/modi-make-in-india-healthcare-digital-mumbai-pm-clean-neonatal-maternal-mortality-224540-2014-10-25.

8 Rao, K. Sujatha. *Do We Care? India's Health System* (New Delhi: Oxford University Press, 2017).

9 https://economictimes.indiatimes.com/news/politics-and-nation/prime-minister-narendra-modi-ensures-ministers-take-decisions-faster/articleshow/35912644.cms?utm_source=contentofinterest&utm_medium=text&utm_campaign=cppst

10 https://economictimes.indiatimes.com/news/politics-and-nation/prime-minister-narendra-modi-ensures-ministers-take-decisions-faster/articleshow/35912644.cms?utm_source=contentofinterest&utm_medium=text&utm_campaign=cppst

11 Prime Minister Narendra Modi at the Inauguration of A.M. Naik Healthcare Complex & Nirali Multi-Speciality Hospital, Narendra Modi, accessed on 3 August 2024, https://www.narendramodi.in/prime-minister-narendra-modi-at-the-inauguration-of-a-m-naik-healthcare-complex-nirali-multi-speciality-hospital-562457.

12 'Government of India Launches "Digital India Initiative"', Press Information Bureau, accessed on 3 August 2024, https://pib.gov.in/newsite/PrintRelease.aspx?relid=110800.

13 "Why India's National Health Insurance Scheme Has Failed Its Poor', *Hindustan Times*, 3 August 2024, accessed on 3 August 2024, https://www.hindustantimes.com/health/why-india-s-national-health-insurance-scheme-has-failed-its-poor/story-6TIXYO0A8CyxTfGYPRdkYK.html.

14 Ministry of Health and Family Welfare, 'Ayushman Bharat: Holistic Healthcare for India', 30 April 2022, https://static.pib.gov.in/WriteReadData/specificdocs/documents/2022/apr/doc202243051901.pdf.
15 'Narendra Modi Quotes: 5 Things PM Said on Launch of Ayushman Bharat Scheme', *Zee Business*, 23 September 2018. https://www.zeebiz.com/india/photo-gallery-narendra-modi-quotes-5-things-pm-said-on-launch-of-ayushman-bharat-scheme-64343
16 Ayushman Bharat: Pradhan Mantri Jan Arogya Yojana. myScheme. (n.d.). https://www.myscheme.gov.in/schemes/ab-pmjay
17 'Ayushman Bharat: Pradhan Mantri Jan Arogya Yojana', myScheme, accessed on 3 August 2024, https://www.myscheme.gov.in/schemes/ab-pmjay.
18 NHA: Official website Ayushman Bharat Digital Mission, NHA, accessed on 3 August 2024. https://abdm.gov.in/.
19 Saurabh Dey, 'Jharkhand Man Praises Ayushman Bharat in Song, PM Modi in Audience', *NDTV*, 18 February 2019, https://www.ndtv.com/india-news/jharkhand-man-praises-ayushman-bharat-in-song-pm-modi-in-audience-1995210.

Chapter 8. The Cultural Reawakening

1 'Nine Years of Modi Govt Have Been in a Way "Cultural Renaissance" for Country: Amit Shah', *The Economic Times*, 6 October 2023, https://economictimes.indiatimes.com/news/politics-and-nation/nine-years-of-modi-govt-have-been-in-a-way-cultural-renaissance-for-country-amit-shah/articleshow/104350291.cms?from=mdr.
2 'Narendra Modi's Varanasi Rally Speech on Dec 20, 2013: Full Text', *India Today*, 17 February 2014, https://www.indiatoday.in/india/narendra-modi-s-speeches/story/narendra-modis-varanasi-rally-speech-on-dec-20-2013-181431-2014-02-17
3 Anil Baluni, 'How the Government Is Bringing Home India's Heritage', Indian Express, March 23, 2023, https://indianexpress.com/article/opinion/columns/

anil-baluni-writes-how-the-government-is-bringing-home-indias-heritage-8873772/.

4 'PM Narendra Modi Will Keep Navratri Fast During US Visit', *The Economic Times*, 25 September 2014, https://economictimes.indiatimes.com/news/politics-and-nation/pm-narendra-modi-will-keep-navratri-fast-during-us-visit/articleshow/43114585.cms.

5 'The Prime Minister, Shri Narendra Modi Addressed the Nation from the Ramparts of the Red Fort on the 76th Independence Day', Press Information Bureau, Government of India,15 August 2022, https://pib.gov.in/PressReleasePage.aspx?PRID=1852024.

Conclusion

1 https://unu.edu/article/how-indias-economy-has-fared-under-ten-years-narendra-modi

Before Modi and After Modi

S.No	Sector	2014	2024
1.	FDI Inflows	$45.14 bn (2014-15)	$667.41 bn (April 2014- March 2024)[1]
2.	Length of Highways	91,287 km (2014)	1,46,145 km (60% growth) (till Nov 2023)[2]
3.	4 lane NH	18,387 km (2014)	46,179 km (till Nov 2023)[3]
4.	Education	Budget- 68,278 crore IITs- 16 (till 2014) IIMs- 13 (till 2014)	Budget- 1.48 lakh crore (2024-25) IITs- 23 (till 2024) IIMs- 21 (till 2024)[4]
5.	Ease of Doing Business Ranking	142	63 (2019)[5]

[1] Press Information Bureau, Government of India, "Make in India- Ministry of Commerce and Industry" (accessed 2024).- https://static.pib.gov.in/WriteReadData/specificdocs/documents/2024/sep/doc2024910391301.pdf

[2] Press Information Bureau, Government of India, Ministry of Road Transport & Highways https://pib.gov.in/PressReleaseIframePage.aspx?PRID=1993425

[3] Press Information Bureau, Government of India, Ministry of Road Transport & Highways https://pib.gov.in/PressReleasePage.aspx?PRID=1988566

[4] Press Information Bureau, Ministry of Education https://pib.gov.in/PressReleaseIframePage.aspx?PRID=2001706 Business Standard, "Budget 2024: Highlights of education budget under Modi govt since 2014" https://www.business-standard.com/budget/news/budget-2024-highlights-of-education-budget-under-modi-govt-since-20 14-123122900689_1.html

[5] Press Information Bureau, Ministry of Finance, Government of India https://pib.gov.in/Pressreleaseshare.aspx?PRID=1601259

6.	UPI transaction	0	Rs 200 lakh crore[6]
7.	Health	Budget- 33,278 crore AIIMS- 7	Budget- 90,958 AIIMS- 23 (till Feb 2024)[7]
8.	**Technology** Increase in Startup Ecosystem	542 (registered firms) (2016)	1.40 lakh startups (as of 30 th June 2024)
	% of people using Digital transaction	7% (2013)	40% (2022)
	Progress of Optical Fibre Deployment	350 km (2014)	6,00,898 km (Oct 2022)[8]
9.	Agriculture	Budget- Rs 13,581 crore	Budget- Rs 1.52 lakh crore[9]
10.	Tourism	Budget- Rs 1,357.30 crores	Budget- Rs 2,479.62 crores[10]
11.	**Defence** Indigenisation and R&D-	Rs 41,906.87 crore	Rs 80,733.54 crore
	Defence Export	Rs 686 crore (2013-14)	Rs 21,083 crore (2023-24)

6 Press Information Bureau (PIB) Report on UPI Growth – A comprehensive document on UPI's progress.

7 Press Information Bureau (PIB) - Health Ministry Budget The Siasat Daily Medical Dialogues - Health Budget Highlights 2024

8 https://indianstartupnews.com/news/india-marked-14-lakh-registered-startups-up-ahead-of-gujarat-and-closer-to-delhi-6705988
Press Information Bureau, Government of India, Ministry of Commerce and Industry
https://indianstartupnews.com/news/india-marked-14-lakh-registered-startups-up-ahead-of-gujarat-and-closer-to-delhi-6705988
https://pib.gov.in/PressReleaseIframePage.aspx?PRID=2004641

9 Press Information Bureau, Government of India, Ministry of Agriculture
https://pib.gov.in/PressReleaseIframePage.aspx?PRID=2035886
Press Information Bureau, Research Unit
https://static.pib.gov.in/WriteReadData/specificdocs/documents/2024/aug/doc2024823379701.pdf

10 Ministry of Tourism, Government of India, "Annual Reports" (2019 and 2024)
https://tourism.gov.in/media/annual-reports

11 Press Information Bureau, Ministry of Defence, Government of India, "Annual Reports" (2013-14 and 2023-24)
https://pib.gov.in/Pressreleaseshare.aspx?PRID=2030887

	Defence Production	Rs 46,429 crore (2013-14)	Rs 1,27,265 crore (2023-24)[11]
12.	Development of NE States Prosperity Through Peace Accords and Gradual Phasing Out of AFSPA	Insurgency-related Incidents- 12,257 Death of Armed Personnel- 526 Death of Civilians- 3479 (2013-14)	Insurgency-related Incidents- 3037 Death of Armed Personnel- 126 Death of Civilians- 413 (2021-22)[12]
13.	Metro network	248 Km (until December 2013)	945 km (until March 2024)[13]
14.	Budget Allocation for the Ministry of Road Transport and Highways	Rs. 31,302.14 (2013-2014)	Rs. 2,78,000 (2024-2025)[14]

[12] Ministry of Home Affairs, Government of India, "Annual Reports" (2013-14 and 2021-22)
https://www.mha.gov.in/sites/default/files/2024-09/NE_MajorInitiativesPeace Process_10092024.pdf
https://static.pib.gov.in/WriteReadData/specificdocs/documents/2023/may/doc202353193801.pdf
https://pib.gov.in/FeaturesDeatils.aspx?NoteId=151186&ModuleId+=+2&reg=3&lang=1

[13] Press Information Bureau, Government of India, Ministry of Housing and Urban affairs
https://pib.gov.in/PressNoteDetails.aspx?NoteId=151870&ModuleId=3

[14] Press Information Bureau, Government of India, Ministry of Road Transport & Highways Budgetr Allocation
https://pib.gov.in/PressReleaseIframePage.aspx?PRID=1988566

15.	Comparison Of Total Length Of Roads Completed Under PMGSY (FY 2013-14 vs FY 2023-24)	PMGSY I - 15,26,484 KM(Sanctioned) 3,81,315 KM (Completed) PMGSY II - 10,632 KM (Sanctioned) 0 KM (Completed)	**PMGSY I -** 6,29,959 KM (Sanctioned) 6,22,070 KM (Completed) **PMGSY II -** 49,342 KM (Sanctioned) 48,529 KM (Completed) **PMGSY-III** 1,10,075.4 KM(Sanctioned) 74,027 KM(Completed)[15]
16.	Faster Adoption and Manufacturing of Hybrid & Electric Vehicles (FAME) Scheme	-	**FAME-I (2015-2019)** Total Allocation ₹529 crore Total xEVs Supported 2.78 lakh

[15] Ministry of Rural Development, Government of India, "Pradhan Mantri Gram Sadak Yojana (PMGSY)" https://rural.gov.in/en/press-release/rural-connectivity-under-pradhan-mantri-gram-sadak-yojana-pmgsy

			Total Electric Buses Deployed 465 Total Fuel Saved 5 crore litres Cumulative CO2 Reduction 12.90 crore kg **FAME-II (2019-2024)** Total Allocation ₹10,000 crore Total xEVs Supported 15.5 lakh (planned) Total Electric Buses Deployed 7,000 (Planned) Total Fuel Saved 47,400 crore litres (estimated till 2030) Cumulative CO2 Reduction 84,600 crore kg (estimated till 2030)[16]
17.	Power generation	1,020.2 Billion Units (2013-14)	1,738.828 BU (2023-24)[17]

[16] Press Information Bureau, Government of India, "Fame India Scheme - Ministry of Heavy Industries", Government of India, "Faster Adoption and Manufacturing of (Hybrid &) Electric Vehicles in India (FAME India) Scheme"
https://pib.gov.in/PressReleaseIframePage.aspx?PRID=2001991
https://pib.gov.in/PressReleaseIframePage.aspx?PRID=2001991
https://www.pib.gov.in/PressReleasePage.aspx?PRID=1741569

[17] Central Electricity Authority, Ministry of Power, Government of India
https://powermin.gov.in/sites/default/files/uploads/power_sector_at_glance_Nov_2023.pdf\
https://powermin.gov.in/en/content/overview

18.	National UJALA Achievement	-	LED lights distributed: 36,86,87,558 Tubelights distributed: 72,18,931 Fans distributed: 23,59,290 (as of 05/04/2024)[18]
19.	Budgetary Allocation To Ministry of Youth Affairs And Sports Under	Rs 1,219 Crore (2013-14)	Rs 3442.32 Crore (2024-25)[19]
20.	MGNREGS Number of Person Days generated	220.37 crore (2013-14) 1660 crore (2006-2014)	309.25 crore (2023-24) 2923 crore (2014-2024)
	MGNREGS Minimum Average Notified Wage Rate	₹55 per day (2013-14)	₹79 per day (2024-25)[20]

[18] Press Information Bureau, Ministry of Power, Government of India https://pib.gov.in/PressReleasePage.aspx?PRID=1787594

[19] Ministry of Youth Affairs and Sports, Government of India, "Demand for Grants" https://yas.nic.in/documents/budgets

[20] Press Information Bureau, Ministry of Rural Development, Government of India
https://pib.gov.in/PressReleasePage.aspx?PRID=2068646
https://pib.gov.in/PressReleasePage.aspx?PRID=2068646
https://www.daijiworld.com/news/newsDisplay?newsID=1239017

About the Author

Arjun Singh Kadian is an academic and policy professional based out of offices in Haryana and Delhi. A geologist by training, he graduated from Hansraj College, University of Delhi, and is a gold medallist in his master's degree. In addition to teaching, he has worked at the Haryana chief minister's office and travelled widely across the region to understand its problems and challenges.

Arjun is an alumnus of the Observer Research Foundation, New Delhi, and Zeit-Stiftung, Hamburg, and a fellow at Konrad-Adenauer-Stiftung, Berlin. He is involved in projects with Indic Academy and Rath Foundation and has initiated the Haryana Thinkers Forum. His first book, *Land of the Gods: The Story of Haryana*, was published in 2021 and his second, *Neeraj Chopra: From Panipat to the Podium*, in 2022. Currently, Arjun is associated with the Prime Ministers' Memorial Museum and Library, New Delhi.